Advance Praise for
LEARNING HOW TO LEARN

"The authors' neuroscience-grounded, yet real-life, approach will be of value to learners of any age."
> —Adam Gazzaley, MD, PhD, Professor in Neurology, Physiology, and Psychiatry at the University of California, San Francisco

"In this highly readable and lively book, the authors illustrate how the brain and behavioral dynamics underlie effective learning—and they do so in a way that young learners will find understandable and even entertaining."
> —Robert A. Bjork, Distinguished Research Professor of Psychology at the University of California, Los Angeles

"*Learning How to Learn* shows kids and teens that a little knowledge of how their brain works goes a long way in helping them improve their learning and studying success. This unique book is full of fun learning strategies—I highly recommend it!"
> —Paula Tallal, PhD, Board of Governors Professor Emeritus of Neuroscience at Rutgers University and cofounder of Scientific Learning Corporation

"I devoured *Learning How to Learn* in three sittings (I needed time for diffuse thinking, active recall, and sleep). A terrific book!"
> —Jeff Sandefer, cofounder of Acton School of Business

LEARNING
HOW TO LEARN

How to Succeed in School
Without Spending All Your Time Studying

BARBARA OAKLEY, PhD,
and **TERRENCE SEJNOWSKI, PhD**

with **ALISTAIR McCONVILLE**

with illustrations by **OLIVER YOUNG**

A TarcherPerigee Book

tarcherperigee

An imprint of Penguin Random House LLC
375 Hudson Street
New York, New York 10014

Most TarcherPerigee books are available at special quantity discounts for bulk purchase for sales promotions, premiums, fund-raising, and educational needs. Special books or book excerpts also can be created to fit specific needs. For details, write: SpecialMarkets@penguinrandomhouse.com.

Library of Congress Cataloging-in-Publication Data

Names: Oakley, Barbara A., 1955- author. | Sejnowski, Terrence J. (Terrence Joseph), author.
    McConville, Alistair, author.
Title: Learning How to Learn : How to Succeed in School Without Spending All
    Your Time Studying / Barbara Oakley, PhD, and Terrence Sejnowski, PhD ;
    With Alistair McConville ; With illustrations by Oliver Young.
Description: New York : TarcherPerigee, [2018] | Includes bibliographical
    references and index. |
Identifiers: LCCN 2018018495 (print) | LCCN 2018024504 (ebook) |
ISBN 9780525504467 | ISBN 9780143132547 (paperback)
Subjects: LCSH: Learning strategies—Problems, exercises, etc. |
    Study skills—Study and teaching. | Students—Time management. | BISAC: JUVENILE
    NONFICTION / School & Education. | JUVENILE NONFICTION / Study Aids /
    General. | JUVENILE NONFICTION / Science & Nature / Biology.
Classification: LCC LB1066 (ebook) | LCC LB1066 .O35 2018 (print) | DDC 370.15/23—dc23
LC record available at https://lccn.loc.gov/2018018495
p.   cm.

Printed in Canada
15th Printing

Book design by Sabrina Bowers

CONTENTS

>

A NOTE TO PARENTS
AND TEACHERS

Welcome to our book. You're helping a younger person to learn more effectively, which means we're already on the same team!

Some of the ideas in this book were discussed in Barb's bestselling *A Mind for Numbers*. Many readers felt that the ideas were so simple, and so practically useful, that they should be shared with younger audiences. And we have heard from thousands of people that these ideas are useful for learning all subjects, not just math.

So this book is intended for tweens and teens—although adults will also find a treasure trove of new and practical ideas here. Understanding just a little bit about how the brain works can make learning more fun and less frustrating.

There are several ways to use this book. Some young adults may wish to read it on their own. They can talk with their friends about the key ideas to help cement them in their minds. Some young adults (and adults!) may be tempted to skim through the book, thinking they'll get everything if they just read from cover to cover. Nothing could be further from the truth! Active involvement is key—the exercises are helpful only if they are completed. The book is best read with a notebook at the side, to take notes, answer questions, and make doodles with key insights. With young "skimmers," the more an adult can dip in, question, and interact, the more will be gained.

If you are a parent or grandparent, aunt or uncle, we suggest that your young person might read the book out loud to you. Generally, a half hour of reading at a stretch is a good length. (Younger children may read for a shorter time.) Reading aloud is a fun adventure where you can learn together, as a family.

If you are a teacher, you may wish to read the book together with your students. Or you may have a silent reading period, followed by a shared discussion. You will find that this book gives you a shared vocabulary to help you teach other subjects.

Younger is better when it comes to learning about learning, as it allows for more years to use the tools. It also opens doors for the great new careers that are emerging with modern-day changes.

Thanks for joining us on this learning adventure. Let's dive in!

—*Barb Oakley, Terry Sejnowski, and Al McConville*

CHAPTER 1

THE PROBLEM
WITH PASSION

Hi, my name's Barb. Great to meet you!

I have a secret. When I was growing up, I was sometimes a terrible student. Sure, I was fine in subjects I liked. But otherwise, forget it.

Everybody told me to follow my passion. I figured that meant, *Do what you like, not what you don't like.* That sounded like good advice to me. I *hated* math and science, so I avoided those subjects as if they were poison. When I had to take those courses, I did badly, or I just plain failed.

I'm now a professor of engineering. Surprised? Engineers *need* a deep knowledge of math and science. I'm now really good at math and science, and I love them. How did I do it? I discovered the secrets of learning well.

This is a picture of me—Barb Oakley. I learned that I could learn much more than I'd ever thought I could.

This is a book about how to become a successful learner. It's written for tweens and teens, but the lessons in it apply to everyone. And they relate to all kinds of learning. Whether you are interested in soccer (better known as football around the world!), math, dance, chemistry, riding a unicycle, learning another language, getting better at video games, or understanding the physics of how a ball bounces, this book is for you.

Brains are amazing. They're the most sophisticated gadgets in the universe. They change their structure depending on what you do with them.

Pretty much anyone can do well in any subject if they know more about learning. Your brain is more powerful than you think. You just need to know how to turn on that power. There are simple tricks that can improve your learning whether you're already a good student—or not so good. These tricks can also make your learning more fun. (For example, you're going to meet a few zombies in this book, but don't worry, they're mostly friendly ones who want to help you learn!)

I wrote this book with Professor Terry Sejnowski. Terry knows a lot about brain science—that is, "neuroscience."* Terry's an expert when it comes to learning. He works with other neuroscientists who are helping us to learn better. Professors from other areas like psychology† and education are also discovering a lot about how we learn.

Here's my coauthor Terrence Sejnowski. He's an expert on the brain.

Terry and I want to share lessons from all of these areas. We want to help improve your ability to learn. The lessons backed by science in this book are coming from both Terry and me. Alistair McConville is also an important part of our author team. He has many years of experience teaching young people, so he helped us make our writing less formal and easier to understand.

---

* You may be wondering what the * symbol, which is called an "asterisk," is doing at the end of the sentence. The asterisk is a symbol that indicates there is a "footnote." This means you may wish to look at the bottom of the page for some more information about stuff that's on that page. (So here it is!) Other symbols might be used, like a dagger for a second footnote on a page, or a double dagger for a third footnote. A footnote usually has interesting information that's on a side topic or only useful for a smaller group of readers. You don't *have* to look at the footnote unless you're curious and would like a little more background.

Anyway, this footnote is here in case you aren't sure how to pronounce the word neuroscience: it's "new-row-science."

† Psychology (pronounced "sigh-KOL-odgy") is the science of why we think and behave the way we do. Some jokers like to say that psychology is a science that tells you what you already know, using words you cannot understand. Psychology does indeed use some big words for important ideas. We'll try to translate them for you in this book.

Here's our other coauthor, Alistair McConville. Al has worked with teens for years!

Terry and I *know* it's possible to improve your learning abilities. How do we know? We teach the largest "massive open online course" ("MOOC") in the world. It's called Learning How to Learn. We have had millions of students. Through this course, we have seen all sorts of people make big improvements in their learning skills. It's not a surprise that the course helps. It's based on the best of what we know from research about how we learn. So we know it works!

Even great students can improve their ability to learn. So can those who are not there yet. The techniques and lessons we're going to teach you won't necessarily make learning super easy. But they will leave you with more time to do the things you like, whether it's video games, soccer, watching YouTube, or just hanging out with friends. In fact, you can use these ideas to *improve* your ability to play soccer and video games!

Learning how to learn will make your years in school more fun and less frustrating. We'll give you powerful tools to improve your memory, to get your work done more quickly, and to help you become an expert at whatever subjects you choose. You'll discover fantastic and inspiring insights. For example, if learning is slow and hard for you, you actually have special advantages in the creativity department.

Learning *how* to learn does something more, though. It opens whole horizons for your future. The working world of the future needs creative people who have many different talents. We're here to help you develop the many talents, and the creativity, that lie within you!

How I Changed My Brain

When I was young, I loved animals and handicrafts, but not numbers. I hated them. For example, I was confused by old-fashioned clocks. Why was the hour hand smaller than the minute hand? Weren't hours more important than minutes? So why wasn't the hour hand the biggest? Why were clocks so confusing?

Me at age ten with Earl the lamb. I loved critters, reading, and dreaming. Math and science weren't on my playlist.

Technology was not my friend, either. I couldn't figure out all the buttons on the TV (this was in the days before remote controls). This meant I only watched TV shows when my brother or sister handled the "technical" side of things. So I didn't feel too good about my chances in subjects like math and science.

Some bad luck at home made things worse. When I was thirteen, my father lost his job because of a back injury, and we had to move. In fact, I moved a lot while I was growing up. By the time I was fifteen years old I had lived in ten different places. Each time I started a new school, I had missed a different piece of math. I felt lost. It was like picking up a book and discovering that the chapters were all out of order. It made no sense to me.

I lost all interest in math. I almost took pride in being terrible at it. It was just "who I was." I thought of numbers and equations as deadly diseases—to be avoided at all costs.

I didn't like science, either. In my first chemistry experiment, my teacher gave my partner and me a different substance from the rest of the class. He made fun of us when we tried to make our results match everyone else's.

Luckily, I was better at other subjects. I liked history, social studies, and anything cultural. My grades in these classes helped me to graduate from high school.

Since I didn't get along with numbers, I decided to learn a foreign language. I had grown up around people who spoke only English. It seemed so exotic to be able to speak two languages. But I couldn't afford to go to college. What could I do?

I found out that the military would pay me to learn a new language. So, right out of high school, I joined the army to learn Russian. Why Russian? No particular reason. It just looked interesting.

I studied at the Defense Language Institute in California. They knew the best techniques for teaching a language. Learning a new language didn't come easily for me. I didn't have a good memory, so I had to practice a lot. But gradually, I got better.

I ended up doing well enough that I earned a scholarship (free money for school) to go to a regular, full-scale university. There, I continued to study Russian. I was so excited! I'd followed my passion for learning a new language, and it was paying off for me.

Except.

Disaster Strikes

The military made me an officer in a group called the Signal Corps. This meant I would be working with my old enemy, technology. Radios, cables, and telephones ... I went from being a language expert to feeling like I was back in my high school chemistry class. I was lost.

Then I was sent to Germany to manage a group of fifty soldiers specializing in communications. More technology. I turned out to be terrible at my job. If *I* couldn't set up the communications gear, how could I tell the soldiers how to do it?

The officers working around me with their own groups were very successful. They were engineers, so they were comfortable with technology, math, and science.

At twenty-six, I left the military. Few people wanted to hire me. My language skills were great, but I didn't have any other skills that would help me get a job. I realized that by only following my passion, I didn't have many choices.

Language and culture will always be important. But today, science, math, and technology are also important. I wanted some of the exciting new opportunities these areas offered! But I'd have to retrain my brain to learn math and science to have a chance. Was that even possible for someone like me?

I decided to try.

Rebuilding My Career

I headed back to university to study engineering. I started at the lowest possible level of math—algebra for people who had failed it in high school.

At first, I felt like I was blindfolded. Other students found solutions to problems easily when I didn't. During those first months, I wondered if I'd made the right decision.

If only I'd known then what I know now, it would have been so much easier. Of course, that's what this book is about. We want to share the best mental learning tools, so you don't struggle like I did.

After a few years of college, my career chances improved. I still used my language skills. For example, I worked as a translator on a Russian fishing boat. But I also began to use my new technical skills. I even ended up working as a radio operator at the South Pole Station.

By the way, the South Pole Station is where I met my husband, Phil. Here he is after just ten minutes at minus seventy degrees in a wild wind. I had to go to the end of the earth to meet that man! If I

My husband, Phil Oakley, in Antarctica after 10 minutes outside at -70° Fahrenheit. He's my hero!

hadn't learned how to learn math and science, I never would have met him. We've now been married for nearly thirty-five years. (You'll meet one of our children later.)

Eventually, I graduated with a new degree in electrical engineering. After working for four years as an engineer, I went back to school to get a master's degree in electrical and computer engineering. Then, with several more years of study, I got a degree called a "doctorate" in systems engineering. That's why people sometimes call me "Doctor" Oakley. (But I still prefer "Barb.") I became an expert at complex mathematical equations and scientific concepts. All this from the girl who couldn't work the TV.

I had "rewired" my brain so that I could overcome my weaknesses.

As a professor, I'm now really interested in how people learn. That's how I got to know my coauthor, Terry Sejnowski. We talked a lot with each other about how people learn. And that's how I got to meet our other coauthor, Alistair ("Al") McConville. He has learned how to learn in an unusual way.

We want to share lessons about how *your* brain learns best. These techniques are simple. Lots of talented adults have told us they wish they'd had these easy-to-understand tools when they were younger—it would have made their learning so much easier. It would even have changed the direction of their learning. They didn't realize the power they had within them.

You have a special gift for learning. When you unleash it while you are still young, you will enjoy its effects throughout your life.

It's easy to believe that you should only concentrate on subjects that come easily for you. But my story reveals that you can do well in subjects you don't even like. The truth is, it's okay to follow your passions. But I also found that *broadening* my passions opened many wonderful opportunities. Learning new subjects I didn't think I could do turned out to be an adventure!

People find it hard to believe they can be successful learners if they have trouble with a subject. But neuroscience (that's "brain science") shows that they're wrong. Your brain is like an incredible tool kit. Your job is to learn when, and how, to use those tools. After all, you wouldn't use a hammer to turn a screw.

Anyway, that's enough about me and why Terry, Al, and I have written this book. In the next chapter, I'll show you what's happening when your learning becomes frustrating. There is a simple trick to make your learning easier and happier.

Now You Try! Do a Picture Walk!

I used to go through my textbook page by page. I was trying to make sure I understood all the ideas before I turned the page. Sounds sensible, right?

Don't do this! It was a big mistake.

Instead, when you start a new chapter, go on a "picture walk"* through it. Scan it. Look briefly at all the pictures, captions, and diagrams, but also at the section headings, bold words, and summary, and even questions at the end of the chapter, if the book has them.

It's important to do a "picture walk" through the book to see the pictures and the section headings before you begin reading.

This might seem crazy. You haven't read the chapter properly yet. But you're giving your brain an idea of what's coming. It's a little like watching a preview of a movie, or checking a map before you set off on a journey. You'll be surprised at how spending a minute or two glancing ahead before you read in depth will allow you to organize your thoughts. This works even if you read

---

* This is also sometimes called a "text walk."

on an electronic device. Just bookmark the beginning of the chapter so you can easily return to it.

It's a little like a closet. The picture walk gives you "hangers" where you can organize the information you're reading. Without hangers, the clothes just fall on the floor in a jumble.

Important! Get out a notebook or a piece of paper—as you read the next chapter, take notes, answer questions, and make doodles with key insights. This will help you avoid mindless reading and help glue the new ideas into your brain. Of course, before you begin to read the chapter, be sure to do a picture walk. And try to answer some of the end-of-chapter questions so you have a sense of what you're aiming at in your learning.

If you make a habit of this for each chapter, you will find the book's ideas will be much more powerful in helping you!

CHAPTER 2

EASY DOES IT

Why Trying Too Hard Can Sometimes
Be Part of the Problem

Has your teacher, or your mom or dad, ever told you to *pay attention*? Or to *focus*? You've probably told *yourself* to do it! That's because it's easy to become distracted. Sometimes whatever is going on outside the window seems more interesting than what's right in front of you. You can't help but think ahead to things like friends, or lunch.

Getting distracted is always bad. Right?

Maybe not. Let's see.

Take a look at the chess game in the following picture. Look at the boy on the left. He's playing against the guy on the right. The boy's rude, isn't he? Typical thirteen-year-old. No concentration. (Ever heard adults say things like that? They usually blame it on smartphones.)

Thirteen-year-old Magnus Carlsen (left) and legendary chess genius Garry Kasparov playing speed chess at the "Reykjavik Rapid" in 2004. Kasparov was surprised that Magnus wandered off, looking at other games. Garry Kasparov is one of the greatest chess players of all time. Magnus is not concentrating, so he must have no chance of winning. Right?

Amazingly, Kasparov didn't win the chess match. It was a tie. The world's best chess player couldn't defeat what appeared to be a hopelessly distracted thirteen-year-old.

Surprise! *Sometimes we need to lose concentration so we can think more clearly.* Zoning out occasionally (not all the time) can be useful when you're learning or problem solving.

Soon after this photo was taken, Magnus returned to the table and focused on the game again. He had taken a little break so he could focus better when he returned.

The message of this chapter is that *sometimes* you need to be *less* focused in order to become a better learner. How can that be?

You've Got Two Ways of Thinking!

In the last chapter, I mentioned the word "neuroscience"—the science of the brain. Neuroscientists use new brain-scanning technology to look inside the brain and understand it better.

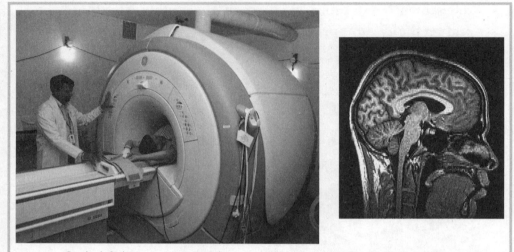

On the left, brain-scanning workers are looking through the scanner. People lie on a special bed that slides into the scanner. The scanner is then able to take a picture of the inside of their brain, like the one on the right. Pretty neat!

Neuroscientists have discovered that your brain works in two different ways. We'll call these two ways of working the *focused* mode and the *diffuse* mode.* *Both* modes are important in helping you to learn.

Focused Mode

When you're using your focused mode, it means that you're paying attention. For example, you might be trying to figure out a math problem. Or you might be looking at and listening to your teacher.

---

* *Diffuse* is pronounced "diff-YOOS." Notice that *focused* has an -ed at the end, but *diffuse* doesn't. The word *diffuse* means "spread out thinly."

You focus when you're playing a video game, putting together a puzzle, or learning words from a different language.

When you're focusing, you're putting specific parts of the brain to work. Which parts are working depends on what you're doing. For example, when you're doing multiplication problems, focusing will use different parts of the brain than when you're speaking.*[1] **When you are trying to learn something new, you must first focus intently on it in order to "turn on" those parts of the brain and get the learning process started.**

When you're in focused mode, you're paying close attention.

Diffuse Mode

If that's *focused* mode, what is *diffuse* mode?

Diffuse mode is when your mind is relaxed and free. You're thinking about nothing in particular. You're in diffuse mode when you're daydreaming or doodling just for fun. If your teacher tells you to *concentrate*, you have probably slipped into diffuse mode.

---

* If you're wondering what that tiny number "1" is doing at the end of the sentence, right after the footnote symbol, it signals an "endnote"—it says there's a note at the end of the book with even more information, usually about the research that relates to the topic. If you want to, take a look at the first endnote at the back of the book. It will help you understand what endnotes do.

In diffuse mode, you're not thinking about anything in particular.

When you're in diffuse mode, you're gently using other parts of the brain that are mostly different from the parts you use when you are focusing. The diffuse mode helps you make imaginative connections between ideas. Creativity often seems to pop out of using the diffuse mode.

It turns out that your brain has to go back and forth between focused and diffuse modes in order to learn effectively.

Let's Play Pinball

To better understand focused and diffuse modes, let's turn to a game called pinball. It's easy to play. You just pull back on a plunger. Once you let the plunger go, it hits a ball up onto a table. You score points as the ball bounces around on the rubber bumpers. Meanwhile, flashing lights and wacky sounds go off. You use the flippers on the lower portion of the table to keep the ball up and bouncing as long as possible.

A pinball machine. You can find video games based on pinball. Even today, it's fun to play!

Pinball tables are kind of like your brain. Their bumpers can be closer or farther apart depending on the table. When the bumpers are close together, it's like your brain in focused mode. The ball bounces around rapidly in one small area before running out of energy and falling down.

Imagine that your mental ball leaves a trail when it travels. That's like your focused mode—you make trails in your brain when you're focused. These trails are laid when you first learn something and begin to practice using it. For example, let's say you already know multiplication. If I asked you to work a multiplication problem, your thoughts would move along the same "multiplication trails" that had already been laid in your brain. To see what I mean, take a look at these pictures.

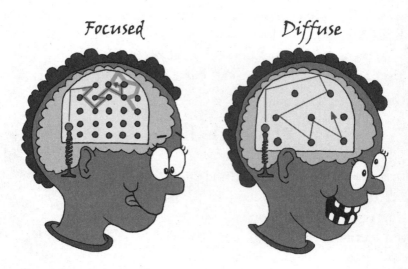

Focused   Diffuse

On the left is the pinball version of the brain in focused mode. See how close together the rubber bumpers are? The ball moves in a tight pattern. Your thoughts can't go very far! The ball is following a fuzzy pattern that has already been laid because you've had the thought before. On the right is a pinball version of the brain in diffuse mode. Notice how widely your thoughts can range in your brain!

The diffuse mode is different. In this mode, the table's bumpers are much farther apart. The thought-ball travels much more broadly around the table, hitting fewer bumpers.

Our brains act like *both* kinds of pinball machine. If we want to shift from thinking about the details to thinking freely about the bigger picture, we have to shift from focused to diffuse mode. You need two tables. (But importantly, your brain can be in only *one* mode at a time. The zombie can't play with two machines at once!)

Here's a fun way to get a sense of the difference between the two modes:

The focused mode—Eyes on the prize!

The diffuse mode—Eyes on the flies![2]

Switching Between
Focused and Diffuse Modes

If switching between modes is so important, how do we do it?

Well, if we want to focus on something, it's easy. As soon as we make ourselves turn our attention to it, the focused mode is *on*. Your thought-ball goes swooshing around on that table. Unfortunately, it's difficult to *keep* our attention on something for long periods of time. That's why we can sometimes fall into diffuse mode and begin daydreaming. As you can see in the picture below, if you let go of the flipper, your thought-ball falls down onto your diffuse table, underneath the focused table.

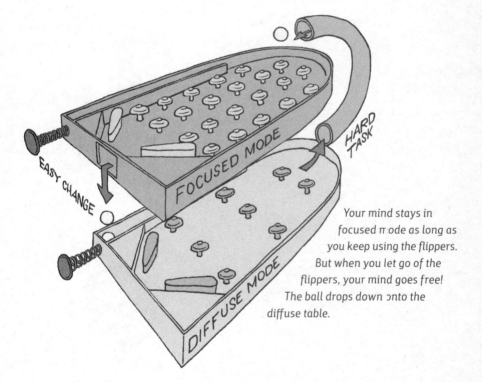

Your mind stays in focused mode as long as you keep using the flippers. But when you let go of the flippers, your mind goes free! The ball drops down onto the diffuse table.

Diffuse mode is when we're not focusing on anything in particular. You can enter diffuse mode by just letting go and *not* concentrating on anything. Going for a walk helps. Or looking out a window from a bus. Or taking a shower. Or falling asleep. (Many famous people have had great insights when the events of the day were sloshing around during sleep.[3])

It also seems that focusing on *something else* can take us temporarily into diffuse mode related to what we're *not* focusing on. When we focus on cuddling our dog, we're not focusing on the math problem. When we're focusing on someone else's chess game, we're not focused on our own chess game. This is why, when you're stuck on a math problem, you can instead switch your focus to studying geography for a while. Then you can make a breakthrough when you return to the math. But it seems that the best ways to give your diffuse mode a chance to work out a difficult problem are through activities like sleeping, exercising, or going for a ride in a vehicle.

Kids with ADHD* sometimes like to imagine that their focused pinball table has a few extra "holes" in it. These holes offer a hidden advantage—they boost creativity! If you have ADHD, the "extra holes" also mean you need to work your mental flippers a little more often than other kids to keep your thought-ball on the focused table.

How do you work the flippers more? Participate as much as you can by asking questions, writing on the chalkboard, distributing activities among your partners, and working with them whenever you have an exercise together.

Kids who have problems paying attention like to imagine that their focused mode has a few extra holes in it. This may mean they have to work their mental paddles harder to get the ball back up into focused mode whenever it might fall out—but it also means they can naturally be very creative. Not a bad trade off!

---

* ADHD means Attention-Deficit/Hyperactivity Disorder. Loosely, it means having challenges with paying attention and controlling impulses. All kids have this to some degree, but with ADHD, it's even more noticeable than usual.

Here's an example to help you feel the shift from focused to diffuse mode.

Use all the same coins to make a new triangle that points
down. You can move only three coins. (You may want to try this by
laying real coins in front of you to see if you can work it out.)

Clue: When you relax your mind and focus on nothing in particular, the solution comes most easily.

Some kids get this exercise instantly, while some professors
just give up because they're focusing too hard.

The solution for this challenge is in the notes section at the
back of the book.[4]

Getting Stuck

There are two ways you can get stuck when you're trying to solve a
math or science problem. Or when you're trying to learn something
new, like how to play a chord on the guitar or perform a specific
move in soccer. The first way you can get stuck happens when you

don't catch the initial explanation. Unfortunately, with this kind of "stuck," going into diffuse mode won't be much use. You haven't "loaded" anything into your focused mode. Your best bet is to go back and look at the examples and explanations in your notes or the book. Or ask the teacher to explain again. Or look on YouTube for an additional explanation. (But don't let yourself get distracted by other videos.)

The second way you can get stuck is when you've studied or focused carefully—you've loaded the explanation into your focused mode. But as you begin to work the problem, play the chord, or make the move, you still find yourself stuck. You grow more and more frustrated. *Why can't you get it?*

It can be easy to get frustrated with your studies.

The reason you get stuck is that you haven't given your brain's diffuse mode a chance to help out! The diffuse mode can't get going until you take your attention *off* what it's focused on. Like Magnus Carlsen, the chess player in the picture a few pages back, sometimes you need to take a break in order to coax your brain's diffuse mode to come to the rescue. Get your mind away from the situation for a while. It opens up your access to the brain's diffuse mode.

Alternatively, focus on something different. For example, if you're working on algebra, you could switch to studying geography. But keep in mind that your brain also needs a little rest sometimes.

If there's something you tend to get stuck at, start with this subject when you are studying. That way you can go back and forth to your other class work over the course of the afternoon and evening when you might find yourself getting stuck. You don't want to leave your hardest subject to the end when you are tired and have no time for diffuse learning.

When you're in diffuse mode, your brain is working on the problem quietly in the background, although you're often not aware of it. The thought-ball in your mind is whizzing around your diffuse mode table, and it can bump into the ideas you need to solve the problem.

When you take a break, how long should it be? This depends on you and how much material you need to cover that day. Five or ten minutes is a good break time. Try not to make your breaks too long. You want to finish so you'll have part of the evening to relax!

Important Learning Tip: Don't Jump to Conclusions about Whether or Not New Learning Strategies Work

Don't try switching just once between focused and diffuse modes while you're studying and then decide that it doesn't work for you. Sometimes you have to go back and forth several times between focused and diffuse to figure something out. You need to focus hard enough on trying to understand the material before you take a break.

How long should you focus? As a rough guideline, if you find yourself stuck after at least ten to fifteen minutes of trying (maybe three to five minutes if you are younger), it may be time for a break. When you do take a break, you need to make sure it's long enough for you to get your mind completely off the material.* It's worth sticking it out and experimenting with the process.

Going back and forth between focused and diffuse modes will help you to master virtually anything, whether it's geometry, algebra, psychology, basketball, guitar, chemistry, or any other subject or hobby you're interested in learning.

Use These Diffuse Mode Tools as Rewards After Focused Mode Work

General Diffuse Mode Activators

> Play a sport like soccer or basketball
> Jog, walk, or swim
> Dance
> Enjoy being a passenger in a car or bus
> Ride a bike
> Draw or paint
> Take a bath or shower
> Listen to music, especially without words
> Play songs you know well on a musical instrument
> Meditate or pray
> Sleep (the ultimate diffuse mode!)

---

* How long it takes can depend on a lot of factors. For example, let's say you have to suddenly get up and give a ten-minute presentation in front of a group. (Surprise!) The excitement and sudden total focus on giving your talk can pull your mind completely off whatever you were working on before. When you return, even after being gone for just ten or fifteen minutes, you can find yourself looking with fresh eyes at whatever you were stuck on. But other times, even several hours isn't enough to really get your mind off it. In that case, a good sleep can work wonders.

The following diffuse mode activators are best used briefly as rewards. These activities may pull you into a more focused mode than the preceding activities. It can sometimes be a good idea to set a timer, or they can eat up too much time.

> Play video games
> Talk to friends
> Help someone with a simple task
> Read a book
> Message friends
> Go see a movie (if you have the time!)
> Watch TV

SUMMING IT UP

Focused and diffuse modes. Our brains operate in two modes: focused and diffuse. You can think of them as pinball tables that have tightly packed bumpers and spread-out bumpers. We need to alternate between these two modes to learn well.

Shifting modes. You shift into focused mode by focusing. Grab those flippers on the pinball machine! But you have to let go and wait for the ball to drop on its own to get into the diffuse mode. The bed, the bath, the bus, and simply going for a walk are great ways to fall into the diffuse mode.

To be a successful problem solver, focus first. We get stuck in problem solving when we don't first prepare our brain by focusing on the basics. Don't just dive into problem solving without studying the explanations first. You need to lay some basic trails on the focused pinball table.

Take breaks to get new problem-solving perspectives. We can also get stuck on a difficult problem even when we've prepared properly. In that case, be a little like the chess-playing Magnus. Wander off for a while and see what else is going on. Take a break. But come back to the game, or you'll lose for sure!

You can choose to go into focused mode. But the diffuse mode is trickier to fall into—the bed, the bath, and the bus, or simply walking, are great ways to summon this more relaxed state of mind.

CHECK YOUR UNDERSTANDING

See how well the key ideas of this chapter have crept into your brain by writing down your answers to the following questions. When you're done, you can compare your answers with the ones at the back of the book.

EASY DOES IT

You may think you can skip these questions, but if you do, you will begin to lose the benefits of this book.

1. What does it mean to be in *focused* mode?

2. What is *diffuse* mode? And what are your favorite diffuse activities?

3. How does a pinball machine (or two) help you understand how your brain works?

4. What is another metaphor for *focused* and *diffuse* modes?

5. What are the two different ways you can get stuck when you are solving a math and science problem?

6. What's the one study habit that you would change as a result of reading this chapter?

Did you do a picture walk yet of the next chapter? Did you try to answer a few end-of-chapter questions? Do you have a notebook out? (Check this off when you're done!) ☐

CHAPTER 3

I'LL DO IT LATER, HONEST!

Using a Tomato to Beat Procrastination

Back in the 1800s, murderers used to love a chemical called arsenic. (It's pronounced "ARE-suh-nick," and sounds like "parsnip.") Arsenic poisoned and killed victims in a day. Painfully.

In 1875 two men ate arsenic in front of an audience. People expected them to die. But to everyone's surprise, they returned the next day, alive and well. How was that possible? How can something so harmful appear to do no damage?

It was a mystery.

We'll tell you later how the story of the arsenic eaters ended, but . . . spoiler alert: It didn't end well for them.

Arsenic is bad for us, but tomatoes are good, right? They are full of healthy nutrients. I'm going to show you how even a plastic tomato can be good for you. It can help you learn better. Sound crazy? All will soon become clear. But don't eat any plastic tomatoes. That's not the trick . . .

The Problem with Putting Things Off

I want to tell you about procrastination.* **Procrastination means putting things off until later.** It is a problem for many students (and adults!) and gets in the way of good learning. Procrastination can be a natural thing to do. Why would you do something you don't feel like doing? Especially if you know it's going to be hard? Why study on Monday when the test is not until Friday? Won't you forget it by then anyway?

Here's the problem. If you procrastinate, you often run out of time. As you will learn later, time and practice work together to help you cement new ideas into your brain. If you run out of time, you not only can't build learning structures, you also spend energy worrying about it. That's a lose-lose situation. Procrastination is the enemy of high-quality learning. But many students still do it. I want to show you how to beat it.

Here's the good news. Your inner zombies are going to help you learn. Now don't freak out. I don't mean you have real zombies inside your skull. That would be gross. But it's nice to imagine an army of tiny zombies up there, working hard for you. You want to make friends with them.

So, we need a pinball machine, a headful of friendly zombies, and a plastic tomato? Who knew? Stay with me . . . I'm a professor!

Distraction and Procrastination

Procrastination is a major problem. We have so many distractions. I always think, "Before I start my homework, I'll play a video game." Before I realize it, I have wasted an hour. I need to find a way to focus on my homework. I should not be waiting until the last minute to do everything.

—*A math student*

---

* It's pronounced "pro-KRAS-ti-NAY-shun." The last part rhymes with "nation."

Procrastination and Pain

Do you groan when your mom or dad tells you to clean, or practice an instrument, or start your homework? This is because when you think about opening that book, or cleaning up, it actually hurts— researchers can see an area of the brain that experiences pain, the insular cortex, begin to light up. To your brain, thinking about cleaning your room feels like the start of a stomachache. But here's what's interesting. Once you get started on the task you didn't want to do, the pain goes away after about twenty minutes. The insular cortex calms down when you start the task you were avoiding. It's happy that you're finally getting on with the job.

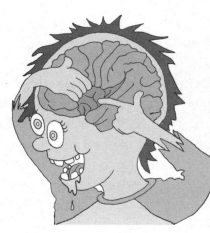

When you even just think about something you don't like, it activates a pain center of the brain called the insular cortex. This can lead to procrastination. (The helpful zombie here is showing you the location of the insular cortex.)

So this is my number one top tip to become a good learner. Just get going. Don't put work off until later.

Easy for the professor to say, you're thinking. How can I change my habits? I'm so used to them.

The answer is . . . a tomato!

The Pomodoro Technique

Has she gone crazy? you ask. How can a tomato make me a better learner?

In the 1980s Francesco Cirillo came up with a way to help procrastinators. It's called the Pomodoro Technique.

Pomodoro is Italian for "tomato." Cirillo developed a tomato-shaped timer, like the one here. Cirillo's technique is simple, and it works. (Terry and I know. It is one of the most popular techniques in our course Learning How to Learn.)

A Pomodoro timer

First, you need a timer. The tomato-shaped timer is great, but any timer will do. I have a digital timer on my computer. Many people use Pomodoro apps on their smartphones or iPads.

The technique works like this:

1. **Shut off all distractions**—your phone, the TV, your music, your brother. Anything that gets in the way of your ability to focus. Find a quiet place to work where you won't be interrupted. If you can afford them, consider noise-canceling earphones or cheaper but just-as-effective earmuffs or earplugs.

2. Set the timer for **25 minutes.***

3. Get going, and **focus** on the task as well as you can. Twenty-five minutes is not long. You can do it!

4. Now for the best part. After 25 minutes, **reward** yourself.

---

* If you are ten to twelve years old, you may want to start with ten- or fifteen-minute Pomodoros.

Watch a dance video or listen to your favorite song. (Maybe dance to it yourself!) Cuddle with your dog. Or chat with friends for five or ten minutes or so. The reward is the most important part of the whole Pomodoro process. When you're looking forward to a reward, your brain helps you focus better.

When you're done with your Pomodoro, reward yourself!

We're going to call this whole process, including the reward, "doing a Pomodoro."

When you "do a Pomodoro" forget about *finishing* the task. Don't say, "I'm going to finish all my homework during this Pomodoro." You *might* finish whatever you're working on. But don't worry about it if you don't. Just work as hard as you can for 25 minutes. When the timer goes off, take a break. Dip into your diffuse mode with that reward.

You may need to do another Pomodoro later, but that's okay. You're doing the right thing just by working hard on the task. Don't worry about how much you do. You will finish. But leave yourself plenty of time. Don't wait until the last minute.

When I do a Pomodoro, my thoughts sometimes wander off. That's perfectly normal. As soon as I catch my thoughts wandering, I just bring them back to the task. It's only 25 minutes, after all. Anyone can do 25 minutes of studying. If I find my thoughts wandering to other tasks I want to do, or websites I want to check, I make a note on a piece of paper so I won't forget, and then I continue with the Pomodoro.

I'll admit that if I *want* to keep working after the time is up, I go ahead. Getting into the flow, where I'm really into doing the task, is a good thing. But when I stop, I always reward myself. It's diffuse mode time! If I've been writing (like this book), I listen to a favorite song. Or I get up and make a cup of tea and look out the window. I don't write during my break. That way, the "writing" part of my brain gets a rest.

It's a good idea to do something during your break that's very different from what you have been focusing on. You want to give a rest to the area of your brain that's been doing the focusing. If you've been sitting while you study, breaks where you move your body around are often the best.

Some people like Pomodoro timers that make a ticking sound. This reminds them that time is passing and they are getting closer to their break. The ticking keeps them focused.

How many Pomodoros should you do in a day? That depends on you. If you're pretty self-motivated and just need an occasional poke to get going, try doing just one or two Pomodoros a day, when you need them. Some people keep careful count of how many Pomodoros they do in a day—they often use Pomodoro apps that collect the day's Pomodoros, kind of like badges. Look up Pomodoro apps and find one that you like—one of the most popular ones we know of is called "Forest."

By the way, don't switch between tasks when you're doing your Pomodoro. Pick a task and work at it until the bell rings. (Of course, if you *finish* a task during a Pomodoro, you can start another.) Some students think they can do several tasks at once, or switch back and forth between several tasks at once. This is called multitasking. But the idea of multitasking is a mistake. Your focus can only be on one thing at a time. When you switch your attention, you waste mental energy, and you will perform worse. It's like a pinball machine where two balls have been released instead of one, and you have to crazily try to manage both the balls. You inevitably fail and both balls drop.

Learning Tip: Set a Timer for Your Breaks—
and Learn to Put Off Your Procrastination!

Just as the Pomodoro timer can be useful for your studies, it can also be useful for relaxing. Set your timer for five, ten, or however many minutes make sense for a break. Remember—taking a break is important so your diffuse mode can help your learning!

For some people, it takes practice to get used to coming back to a task after a break ends. A break timer that has a very distinct and loud sound can be useful here.

Sometimes people find it hard to stop procrastinating. If that's the case, a good mental trick is to tell yourself that you're going to procrastinate *ten minutes later*. Meanwhile, during those ten minutes, look at (or make) a list of what you plan to do. This will allow your diffuse mode to start thinking in the background about your tasks and how you're going to get them accomplished.

Good Zombies and Bad Zombies

This takes me back to zombies. Sometimes they have a bad reputation. People think of them as monsters—scary-looking creatures who are under the control of something or someone else.

But zombies (at least in our book!) are just your habits. There are good, neutral, and bad zombie habits. (Okay, maybe the bad zombies really aren't that bad—they're just not helpful sometimes.)

What do all zombies have in common? They work automatically toward their goal (which generally involves eating brains). Nothing distracts them. They never give up. It's like they're on autopilot.

Your habits are like zombies—you can have bad ones or good ones.

We all have a zombie mode—fortunately, it usually doesn't involve eating weird substances, like with real zombies. We do things automatically because we've done them so many times before. What are your zombie mode habits? Throwing your shoes down as you come in from school? Falling into a favorite chair in front of the TV? Or reaching for your phone as soon as it vibrates? No thinking. No discussion. That's you in zombie mode.

Imagine being as focused as a helpful zombie on your studies during the time you're supposed to be studying. Practicing the Pomodoro Technique will help you get there. But you need to defeat your bad zombie habits on the way.

Studying and texting in the same time frame is a bad habit. It's your bad "study while texting" zombie. To defeat it, you can instead train a helpful zombie—get used to turning your phone off, silencing it, or leaving it in another room. The new good zombie can allow you to overcome the bad one!

If your brother interrupts you, train your helpful inner zombie to tell your brother you're "doing a Pomodoro." Ask your brother to stay away until you've finished. If you know you get hungry, have a snack *before* you do a Pomodoro. Instead of mindlessly jumping into a new chapter of your textbook, first do a picture walk, and then take notes on the paper that your good zombie mode has thoughtfully placed beside you. Replace your bad zombie habits with ones you know will make things better for you.

Back to the Arsenic Eaters

Remember the arsenic eaters? How did they eat arsenic and not die on the spot? And what does eating a deadly poison have to do with something as seemingly harmless as putting things off—procrastination?

The arsenic eaters ate a little bit of poison each day. They trained their bodies to expect it. They were building up an immunity. They thought they were getting away with it because they didn't feel ill.

They didn't realize it, but they were gradually poisoning themselves.

A little bit of arsenic won't kill you right away. But it's very unhealthy. Over time it does serious damage—cancer and other damage to your internal organs. Don't eat arsenic!

How is this like procrastination?

It doesn't seem like it hurts if you put off your studies a little longer. Or spend another "few minutes" on social media. But if you get used to procrastinating, it will make learning harder, because you will have less time when you do buckle down to learn. You'll get stressed, miss deadlines, and not learn things properly. You can get really behind. All this will make you a less effective student.

Remember, you can build an army of helpful zombies up there, working hard for you if you make short periods of focused concentration into a habit. So learn to love that plastic tomato! Or the Pomodoro app on your phone.

Now You Try! Preplanning to Avoid Distraction

Write down the things that distract you from the task at hand. For each one, come up with a new habit to work on. (If you're reading this on an electronic device, make your own table on paper.) Here's an example to get you started. If you are younger, you may want to sit down with an adult for ten minutes or so to get you started.

DISTRACTION: Bad Zombie	SOLUTION: Friendly Zombie
My phone vibrates— I stop working.	Leave phone on the kitchen table when doing a Pomodoro.

Now You Try! Boost Your Reading Power with Active Recall

We want to give you a sneak preview now of an important learning technique that will help you in the chapters ahead. This technique is called *active recall*. Active recall means bringing an idea back to mind. *Actively recalling* key ideas you are learning has been shown to be a great way to understand them.[1]

You can probably guess that we've been teaching you how to avoid procrastination so you have more time for important techniques like active recall.

Here's how you do it. Before you begin to read a chapter in a book, first do a picture walk through it. (We talked about this at the end of the first chapter.)

Then begin reading. Don't rush. Go back over a paragraph if it doesn't make sense to you or if your attention wanders. (Wandering attention is perfectly normal. It doesn't mean you're not smart enough.) Jot a few words in the margin or on another sheet of paper about an idea you think is important. If you need to, underline a key word or two, but not too many.

This is the critical part. Look away from the page and see what you can recall. What are the key ideas on the page? Play them back in your mind. Or say them out loud to yourself. Do not simply reread the page over and over again. And don't underline or highlight big amounts of text.

Pulling the key idea from your own mind, instead of just reading or rereading it on the page, is the critical idea behind active recall. You don't need to use recall with every page of the book. But if you try it on a few key pages, you'll be surprised at how this can help.

Research has shown that if you use active recall in your studies, you will do much better later when you are taking tests. Using recall in your learning means you can perform well even when you're under stress.[2] And it doesn't just put information into your memory—it also builds your understanding.[3]

The Three Key Steps to Powerful Reading

1. Picture walk

2. Read with care

3. Use active recall

You can also use active recall as a great general learning tool. For example, close this book and see how many key ideas you've read so far that you can remember. Once you've done your best, open the book back up and see how it compares!

Recall the information at different times and in different places. You can use active recall while waiting for a friend, sitting on a bus, or before going to sleep. There are two important reasons to use recall in this way. First, you don't have your notes or the book in front of you, so you are truly recalling the information, rather than sneaking a peek. Second, you don't have your usual study environment around you. As you'll see later, learning in different places can glue the information more strongly in your mind.

When I was in middle school, I used to walk to my grandma's house for lunch. As I was walking, I would try to recall key ideas that I'd just learned in the class, as if rewatching an interesting film. This technique helped me tremendously to excel in my studies.

—*Zhaojing "Eileen" Li, graduate of Tsinghua University—China's top university*

SUMMING IT UP

> We all develop habits. They're our inner zombies. Things we do without even thinking about them.

> **Our zombie habits can be helpful or not.** Some are great time savers. But often people develop the habit of putting off their work—procrastination. This is really bad for effective learning. It doesn't leave you enough time to focus or to soak in the lessons you've learned.

> Luckily you can change your habits and make them stick. **The Pomodoro Technique is a great way of helping you to do focused work.** Make a habit of it. Shut off distractions and set a timer to work for 25 minutes. Easy. Then take a break and reward yourself. Do something "diffuse."

> **When you put something off, it's hurting your brain.** Just getting going stops the suffering.

> *Active recall* **is a powerful technique for learning.** Pull key ideas *from your own mind* to review them. Don't just look at a page or your notes and fool yourself into thinking that the information is in your head.

CHECK YOUR UNDERSTANDING

To make sure you've got the hang of this chapter, answer the following questions. Say the answers out loud to yourself or write them down or try to *teach* someone else the answers by explaining what you have learned.

When you're done, you can compare your answers with the ones at the back of the book.

1. What is procrastination?

2. Why is procrastination bad for your learning?

3. What happens in your brain when you think about something you don't like or don't want to do?

4. How would you explain the Pomodoro Technique to someone who had never heard of it?

5. What is the most important part of the whole Pomodoro process?

6. What should you do during your break between Pomodoros?

7. Should you plan to finish a task during a Pomodoro? Why or why not?

8. What can be good about going into zombie mode?

9. What does zombie mode have to do with procrastination?

10. What was the point of the arsenic eaters story? How does it link to procrastination?

11. Explain the idea of *active recall*.

Picture walk done, a few end-of-chapter questions tackled, and notebook ready for the next chapter? ☐

CHAPTER 4

BRAIN-LINKS AND
FUN WITH SPACE ALIENS

Santiago was eleven years old and in trouble. Big trouble. This time, he landed in jail.

He'd had it coming. Santiago argued endlessly with his father and fought with his teachers. He was kicked out of school, time after time. But this time, he had blown a hole in a neighbor's gate with a homemade cannon!

He hated school. He didn't have a good memory, which made it hard for him to learn in exactly the way teachers wanted him to learn.* He especially hated math and didn't see the point. He liked to draw, but his father thought drawing was useless.

Santiago was going nowhere fast. But guess what? Santiago eventually won a Nobel Prize—that's like an Olympic gold medal for science! He became the father of modern neuroscience. "Bad boy" Santiago Ramón y Cajal† became one of the greatest scientists of all time.[1] He used art skills *and* math skills.

We're going to tell you how it happened. But first, let's learn a

---

* It's important to make something clear here. Santiago didn't just *think* he had a lousy memory—he actually *had* a lousy memory, as he described in detail in his autobiography. This means if you have a not-as-good-as-average memory, and you sometimes struggle with learning, there's still lots of hope for you! More about this later.

† It's pronounced "ra-MON-ee-ka-HALL."

little about the brain. This will allow you to understand one of Santiago's breakthrough discoveries. It will also help you understand how we learn!

Friendly Space Aliens: How Neurons "Talk"

Let's start with a few simple ideas about the brain.

Your brain has a lot of neurons in it. Billions, roughly the same number as the number of stars in the Milky Way galaxy. Neurons are the building blocks of your brain. They're small. Really small. Ten neurons are only as wide as a human hair! But they can be long—longer than your arm.

To understand neurons, you can think of tiny aliens from outer space.

Yes, aliens. Can you see the eye of the neuron-alien below? (Technically, the eye is called the *nucleus*—there is a nucleus in every cell in our body.) The neuron-alien's single arm stretches above, almost like a hat. The neuron-alien's three legs are underneath.

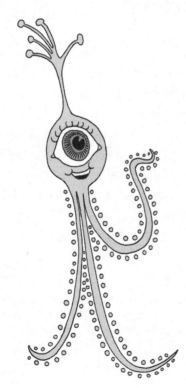

A neuron-alien—
our metaphor for a real neuron.

Neuron-aliens are bizarre creatures. They have only an eye, one arm, and three legs. (In real life, neurons can have more than three "legs." Lots more! They come in many shapes and sizes, with more variety than all the other types of cells in your body.)

Below is a drawing that is much closer to the look of a real neuron. Down below are the neuron's "legs." They're called *dendrites*. Up above is the neuron's "arm." It is called an *axon*.*

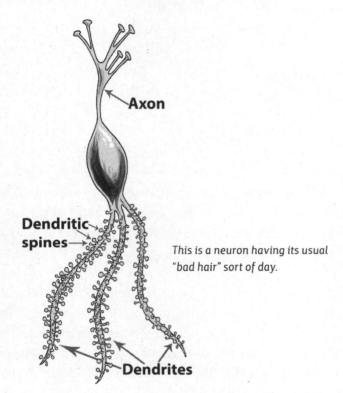

This is a neuron having its usual "bad hair" sort of day.

Look at those knobby spines on the dendrite "legs" of the neuron. Those are called *dendritic spines*. They are like toes scattered all over the space alien's legs. (Remember. This is an *alien*. It doesn't look like we do!)

---

* The "fingers" at the end of the axon arm are called *boutons*. In a neuron that sends a signal to another neuron, the first neuron's bouton snuggles against a dendritic spine of the second neuron. The two neurons are separated only by the synaptic gap. In this way, the bouton and the dendritic spine are like a married couple that can send "kisses" to one another across the synaptic gap.

Dendritic spines may be tiny, but they are important. You'll see them again in some unexpected places in this book.

Here's a key point: Neurons send signals to other neurons.

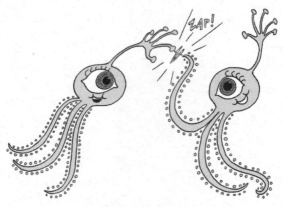

What's new, Ron?

It's easiest to understand this by returning for a moment to our space aliens. When one neuron-alien wants to "talk" to the next alien, it reaches its arm out and gives the tiniest of shocks on the toe of the next alien. (These particular aliens show friendship by giving tiny shocks to one another. Weird, I know.)

It's similar for real neurons. A neuron ripples a signal along its axon to cause a shock in a dendritic spine of the next neuron.[2] It's like the tiny shock you feel with static electricity on a dry day. One neuron sends a shock across a tiny, narrow gap to another neuron. This gap is called a *synapse*. (It's pronounced "SIN-naps" in the United States and "SIGH-naps" in England.)

There. You've just understood the process of how a neuron passes along a signal! Okay, maybe it's more complicated than that—there's some chemistry involved. But you now understand the basics.

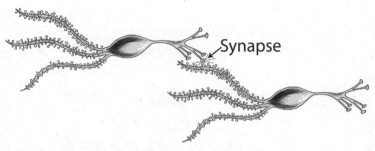

Synapse

Two neurons connect together across a synapse.

You can also see a close-up view of a synapse. The "spark" from the synapse creates an electrical signal that can flow through the neuron. If the signal reaches the end of the axon, it can cause a spark in the next neuron. And the next. And the next.* *These flowing signals are your thoughts.* They're like the trails on your mental pinball table.

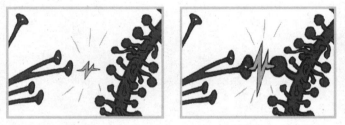

On the left is a close-up of a small synapse. See the little "spark"?
On the right is a bigger synapse that has grown because of practice.
See how much bigger the spark is?

---

* We've made things sound pretty simple here. But it's a little like a conversation at a dinner party—there can be complicated maneuvering going on behind the scenes. A signal can indeed pass from a dendrite on through the cell body to the axon, and then on to the next neuron's dendrite. But at every step of the way, the progress of the signal depends on many different factors, like where the dendritic spine is located on the dendrite, and how many other signals are arriving at the neuron.

The arrows in the picture below show how a signal could flow through the synapses and the neurons.

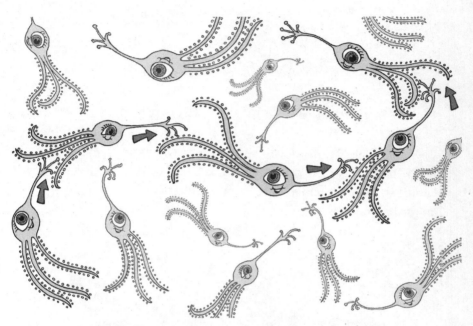

Signals flow across neurons—these create your thoughts!

Let's return again to our friends the neuron-aliens. The more often a neuron-alien shocks the next neuron-alien so that it passes the message on to its friends, the stronger the connection between them becomes. The neuron-aliens are like friends who become better friends because they talk a lot.

It's like that for real neurons, too. Researchers often use the phrase "Neurons that fire together, wire together."[3] You can think of the "wiring together" as creating a *set of brain-links*. Learning something new means creating new or stronger links in your brain. A new set of brain-links![4]

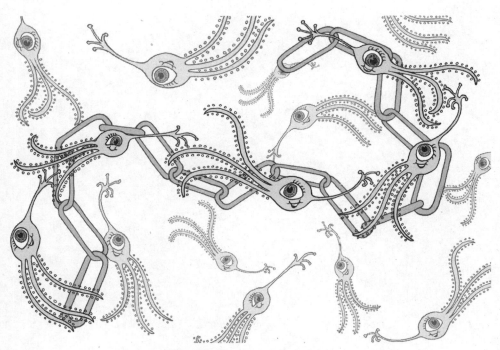

A weak set of links forms when you begin to learn something.

When you first learn something new, the brain-links are weak. There may be only a few neurons linked together. Each neuron may have only a small dendritic spine and a small synapse. The spark between the neurons isn't very big.

As you practice a new idea, more neurons join in.[5] And the synaptic links between the neurons get stronger. This means the sparks get bigger. More neurons, stronger synapses—the brain-links get stronger, too![6] Longer brain-links can store more complex ideas. The opposite happens when neurons don't fire together—their connections weaken, just like two friends who don't talk anymore.

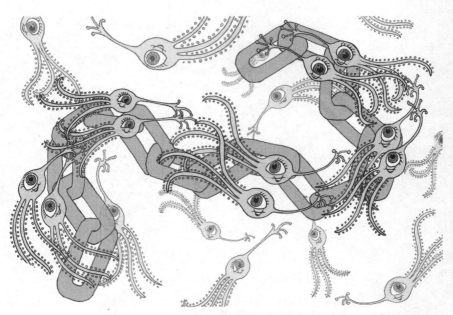

The more you practice, the stronger your set of brain-links gets.[7]

Some people like to think of a set of brain-links as if they were paths that a mouse runs along in a forest (the mouse is like the bouncing "thought-ball" in the pinball machine metaphor). The more times the mouse runs along the pathway, the clearer the path becomes. The wider the path is, the easier it is to see and follow it.

So then, what's the mouse metaphor for the diffuse mode? Simple. In the diffuse mode, the mouse—the thought—doesn't run along the path. Instead, the thought-mouse jumps onto a tiny drone and flies to its new location!

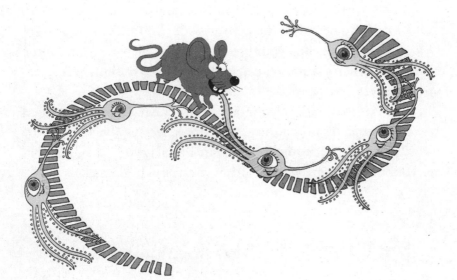

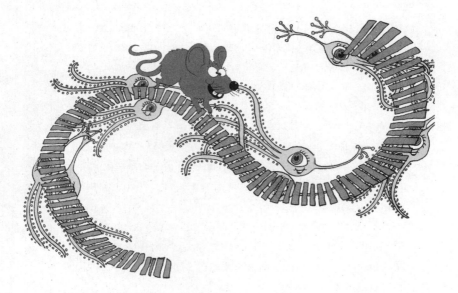

Neural paths get wider and easier to travel on the more your mental "mouse" runs along the path.

Don't worry that you might accidentally use up all your neurons while you're making bigger and wider brain-links. You've got *billions* of neurons—and your brain is growing new neurons all the time. More than that, you can make billions and billions of connections *between* neurons!

The fact that trails in your brain can change and grow is called *neuroplasticity*. (It's pronounced "new-row-plas-TI-sity.") This fancy word just means that your neurons are like clay you can mold. That is, your neurons can change. This is why *you* can change!

Now You Try! Make Your Own Neurons

You can make your own neurons and brain-links. The simplest approach to making a model set of brain-links is to take a strip of construction paper and glue the ends together. Then, take a new strip and thread it through the first one (now a closed circle). Then glue the ends of the second strip together. This can be repeated until your number of "brain-links" reaches its desired length.

More advanced crafters can use pipe cleaners and beads of different sizes—making sure that the pipe cleaners can fit through the beads. Use the pipe cleaners to form the axon, the boutons (which are the "fingers" at the end of the axon), the dendrites, and the dendritic spines. The small balls on the ends of the dendritic spines can be represented by the small beads. The neuron's "eye" (the nucleus) can be a larger bead.

Making your own neurons is a great way to remember all the different parts. By lining your neurons up, axon to dendrite, you can better understand how the neurons "talk" to one another.

A Neuron Mystery

Back when Santiago Ramón y Cajal was around, in the late 1800s, scientists didn't know that the brain was made of individual neurons. Scientists thought that maybe neurons joined to one another to form a network. This network was spread throughout the brain, like a spiderweb.* Scientists believed the brain was a single, spiderweb-like network of neurons because electrical signals flowed so easily between different parts of the brain. How could signals flow so easily if they had to jump from one neuron to another neuron?

The problem was that it was hard to see what was going on. Microscopes weren't good enough to see whether there were any gaps between neurons. The spiderweb theory seemed reasonable at the time. But Santiago thought that there were special gaps between neurons. He believed the gaps were just too small to see. Santiago proposed that signals jumped across the gap a little like an electrical spark. (Similar to how our neuron-aliens send signals by sparking one another!) Santiago was right, of course. Now we can see the synaptic gap with new tools that are better than old-fashioned microscopes.†

Today, neuroscientists can listen to neurons chitchatting in the brain. The electrical waves are easy to see using cool technology like the EEG.‡ It's like watching ocean waves swooshing along.

---

* The idea that neurons form one single network was called the "reticular theory." This contrasted with Santiago's idea, that there were many smaller neurons that sent signals to each other across tiny gaps. Santiago's idea was called "neuron theory."

† Not all synapses have a gap, though. Some neurons do have a direct electrical connection. These direct connections are more common early in the development of the cerebral cortex, but most of them disappear in adult brains.

‡ "EEG" stands for *electroencephalogram* (pronounced "elek-tro-en-SEF-a-lo-gram"). This technique uses round metal disks placed around the outside of a person's head to help researchers see the electrical activity in the brain.

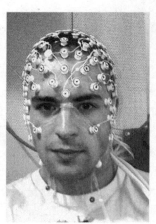

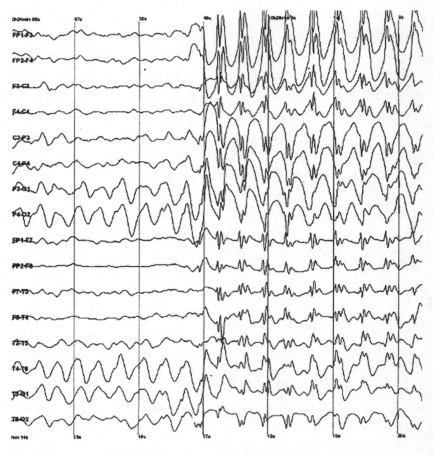

Above is a person with EEG sensors on his head. Below are some of the EEG waves his brain is making.

We Love Metaphors!

Can you tell that we like to use *metaphors*? A metaphor is a *comparison* between two things.* One thing is something you are familiar with, like an ocean wave. The other thing is something you may not be familiar with, like an electrical wave. Metaphors allow you to connect what you already know to the new concept you're learning. This helps you learn faster. (Obviously, an electric wave is not the same as an ocean wave, a neuron is not a space alien, and a dendritic spine is not a toe. They just share some similarities.)

Coming up with a creative metaphor is one of the best ways to learn a new concept or share an important idea. That's why some metaphors have meaning in every language, like the Swahili proverb "Wisdom is wealth." Great writers are known for their metaphors. Have you ever heard Shakespeare's line "All the world's a stage"? You are the actor.

When you think of a metaphor, a trail in your brain is activated. (Yes, this trail is the set of brain-links you saw before.) The trail allows you to more easily do complex thinking about the "real" concept. Just by thinking of a metaphor, you've started understanding the tougher concept! Metaphors help you to *get it* faster. (All this relates to something called the "neural reuse theory."[8] You are reusing ideas you have already learned to assist you in learning new ideas.)

Usually, at some level, a metaphor stops working. For example, space aliens shocking each other is a metaphor that doesn't explain synapses well if you look more closely. When a metaphor doesn't seem to work anymore, you can just throw it away. You can find a new metaphor to assist you in understanding more deeply. You can also use different metaphors to help you understand a single idea. That's just what we've done when we said that a connected set of neurons is like a set of brain-links, or like a mouse path in a forest.

---

* English teachers are very wise with words. They might point out that technically I'm sometimes using an *analogy* or a *simile*, which are similar to metaphors. But just to make things easier for you in this book, I'll stick to using the word *metaphor*.

A metaphor helps you understand a new idea by connecting it to something you already know. Whenever a metaphor doesn't work or breaks down, you can just throw it away and get a new one.

In our book, you'll meet many metaphors: zombies, links, mice, and octopuses. We use the metaphors to give you a better sense of the science. Remember, metaphors are just handy ways of helping you understand key ideas. Don't worry if your metaphor seems strange. Sometimes wackier metaphors open your mind to the new idea you're trying to learn. Wacky metaphors are usually memorable, too!

Now You Try! Understanding a Metaphor

We mentioned two metaphors:

> Wisdom is wealth.
> All the world's a stage.

Take a minute to think about these examples. Is their meaning clear to you? See if you can put these metaphors into other words. If not, you can check the endnotes for an explanation.[9]

Santiago Ramón y Cajal

So how did Santiago become such an incredible scientist?

It wasn't easy.

Santiago's dad realized that his son needed a different approach. His dad got him interested in medicine by showing him what real bodies looked like. How? The pair went off secretly at night to find bodies in graveyards. (This was back in the 1860s. They did things differently back then. Do not try this today!)

Santiago started drawing parts of the body. Being able to see, touch, and draw what he was learning about captured his interest.

Santiago decided to become a doctor. He went back to the mathematics and science studies he had missed when he was young. This time, he paid attention. He worked hard to build the proper trails in his brain that he hadn't built when he was younger.

He finally became a doctor! He was interested in all types of cells. So he decided to try to become a professor of pathology. (That's a professor who is an expert at telling the difference between healthy and sick body tissues. This is done by running tests on them that include looking at them closely through a microscope.) For this, Santiago had to pass an important test. He studied hard for a year. And he failed. So he studied hard for another year. And he failed again. He finally passed on the third attempt.

Santiago Ramón y Cajal, always ahead of his time, shown here around 1870 taking one of the world's first selfies. (Note, you cannot see his right hand because it's pushing the button to take the picture.) Santiago cared a lot about young people. He even wrote a book for them—Advice for a Young Investigator.

Santiago went on to draw beautiful pictures of all the neurons he saw through his microscope. His atlas of neurons is still the starting point for modern studies of neurons.

But there was a problem. Santiago wasn't a genius, and he knew it. He often wished he were smarter. He stumbled over his words, and he forgot details easily. But his research on neurons showed him that he could retrain his brain. Efforts to learn subjects like math and science gradually changed his abilities in those areas. By slow, steady practice, he could make new links—changing the structure of his brain. That's how he changed from a young troublemaker to a famous scientist!

Today's scientific research confirms what Santiago discovered. We can all "think" ourselves smarter. *Learning* makes us smarter. And learning how to learn is one of the best things you can do to get the ball rolling and make learning more successful. This is the most important idea in this book! So keep reading!

Later we'll meet Santiago again. And we'll discover more about why he could outthink geniuses—despite his "limited" brainpower.

Common Excuses in Learning[10]

It's easy to come up with excuses for why good learning techniques aren't for you. Here are the most common excuses—and how you can challenge them.

1. I don't have time.

If you don't take the time to work problems and read more slowly and carefully, you will not be able to grow new neural connections—which is the only way you learn. If you've quickly run your eyes over the material in a book, it's still just lying there on the page. It's not in your brain. *You haven't learned it.* This is why you really need to focus while you're doing a Pomodoro, rereading if necessary. It helps you make the best use of your valuable time.

2. I don't have a good imagination.

Creating metaphors and quirky pictures to help you remember might sound difficult. You may think that you don't have the same imagination that adults have. That's not true! The closer you are in years to your childhood, the more imagination you naturally have. You want to keep that childish imagination and build on it by using your imagination to help you learn.

3. What I'm learning is useless.

We don't normally have to do push-ups, pull-ups, or sit-ups in our everyday lives. But still, those exercises aren't useless—they help keep us in good physical shape. In a similar way, what we learn may be different from what we do in everyday life—but the new learning helps keep us in mental shape. More than that, new learning serves as a resource to help us transfer new ideas into our lives by using metaphor.

4. My teachers are really boring.

Your teachers give you some facts and ideas. But you are the one who must come up with a story that has meaning for you and will help make the concepts stick in your mind. The most boring thing would be if the teacher did all this work for you already, leaving you with nothing to do!

You are a critical part of the learning process. It's important for you to take responsibility for creating your understanding.

Pause and Recall

After you read this "Pause and Recall" section, close the book and look away. What were the main ideas of this chapter? Write down as many ideas as you can—you'll find that your neurons will fire better and you'll remember more easily if you're actively writing.

Don't worry if you can't recall much when you first try this. As you continue practicing this technique, you'll begin noticing changes in how you read and how much you recall. You might be surprised to learn that even distinguished professors will sometimes admit that they have trouble recalling the key ideas of what they've just read!

Check this box when you're done: ❏

Now You Try! Create Your Own Metaphor for Learning

We'd like you to think about your latest learning challenge—whether it's in math, language, history, or chemistry. Try to come up with a good metaphor for what you're learning. Explain your metaphor to one of your friends. Remember—using a metaphor is really just finding a way to connect your new learning to something you already know.

A good way to come up with a metaphor is to take out a sheet of paper and begin doodling. Surprisingly helpful ideas can emerge from silly doodles!

Here are a few examples to get you started:

> If you are learning about electrons, you might think of them as tiny fuzzy balls. Flowing electrons make an electrical current, just like flowing water molecules create a water current.

> You might think of history as having "streams" of different factors that all contribute to historical events like the French Revolution or the development of the automobile engine.

> In algebra, you can think of *x* as being a rabbit that pops out of the hole only when you solve the equation.

Key Terms Related to Neuroscience

Axon: An *axon* is like the "arm" of a neuron. It reaches out toward the next neuron in a *set of brain-links*.

Brain-links: A *set of brain-links* is a term used in this book to indicate neurons that have become part of a team by frequent "sparks" across *synapses*. Learning something new means creating new *brain-links*.

Dendrite: *Dendrites* are like the "legs" of a neuron. The *dendritic spines* on the dendrite receive signals from other neurons and can pass them along the dendrite toward the main body of the cell (the neuron-alien's "eye").

Dendritic spine: *Dendritic spines* are the "toes" that stick out of a dendrite (a "leg" of the neuron). Dendritic spines form one side of a synaptic connection.

Diffuse mode: We use the term *diffuse mode* to mean that certain parts of your brain become active when you're resting and not thinking about anything in particular. (Neuroscientists call this the "default mode network," the "task negative network," or the "activation of neural resting states.")

Focused mode: We use the term *focused mode* to mean that certain parts of your brain go to work when you pay close attention to something. When you are focusing, the active parts of your brain are mostly different from those parts that are active in the diffuse mode. (Instead of "focused mode," neuroscientists use the heavy-duty term "activation of task positive networks.")

Neuron: *Neurons* are tiny cells that are key building blocks of your brain. Your thoughts are formed by electrical signals that travel through neurons. In this book, we say that a neuron has "legs" (dendrites) and an "arm" (an axon), almost like a space alien. An electrical signal can travel from the neuron's legs to its arm, where it can "shock" the next neuron in a set of links.

Neuroplasticity: The fact that trails in your brain can change and grow is called *neuroplasticity.* Your neurons are like plastic clay you can mold. You can change your brain through learning!

Synapse: A synapse is a special, very narrow gap between neurons. Electrical signals (your thoughts) can jump across this gap with the help of certain chemicals. When we say a "stronger synapse," we mean that the effect of the signal jumping across the gap is stronger.

SUMMING IT UP

> Neurons send **signals** that flow through your brain. These signals are your thoughts.

> Neurons have a distinctive look, almost like space aliens. There are **dendrites** ("legs") on one side of the neuron and an **axon** ("arm") on the other.

> *Dendritic spines* are like "toes" on a neuron's "legs."

> **The axon of one neuron "shocks" a dendritic spine on the next neuron.** This is how one neuron sends a signal to the next neuron.

> **The word *synapse* refers to the special narrow gap where the axon and the dendritic spine are nearly touching one another.** A "spark" is sent from the axon to the dendritic spine.

> **Metaphors are powerful learning tools.** They help us reuse neuron trails we have already developed so that we can learn more quickly.

> **If a metaphor is no longer useful, throw it away and get a new one.**

> In our book, we point out that a set of brain-links (or mouse paths) can grow stronger in two ways:

> ▶ **Each synapse gets bigger,** so each spark is stronger.

> ▶ **More neurons join in,** so there are more synapses.

> **You strengthen your brain-links (or mouse paths) by practicing.**

> It's easy to come up with excuses for why good learning techniques aren't for you. **It's important to challenge these excuses.**

> **Even kids who start out badly at school can turn things around and end up being successful.** Remember Santiago Ramón y Cajal, the father of modern neuroscience!

CHECK YOUR UNDERSTANDING

Have the key ideas of this chapter slipped into your brain? Answer the following questions.

1. The _____ that neurons send to other neurons form your _____. (Fill in the blanks with the best words.)

2. From memory, draw a picture of a neuron. Label the key parts. Try to do this first without looking back at the picture. *Active recall* instead of just looking at the answer. That's what helps the new set of brain-links to grow!

3. Does an axon shock a dendritic spine? Or does a dendritic spine shock an axon? In other words, does the signal go

from the axon to the dendritic spine? Or the other way around?

4. What do you do when a metaphor breaks down and doesn't work anymore?

5. Why did scientists think that your brain was made of one single neuron network instead of thinking that there were many smaller neurons that sent signals to each other across tiny gaps?

6. What is a "set of brain-links"?

7. How is a "thought" similar to a mouse in a forest?

8. When you learn something new, you form a new set of _____ in your brain. (Several different words could be used here.)

(When you're done, you can compare your answers with the ones at the back of the book.)

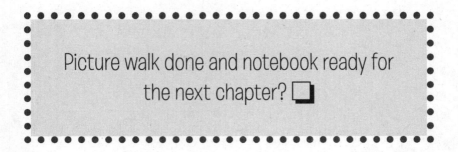

Picture walk done and notebook ready for the next chapter? ☐

CHAPTER 5

THE OTHER SIDE OF
THE TEACHER'S DESK

Hi. I'm Al. Pleased to meet you. I'm helping Barb and Terry
write this book. Sometimes professors use big words and long sentences. I'm here to keep an eye on the language!

I'm forty-two years old, but this summer I found myself sitting
nervously in an exam hall with a group of sixteen-year-old students. I was working on a chemistry test. I was the only adult in
there. Why? Had I been held back twenty-six years? . . .

I'll explain.

I teach at a school in England. It's a really nice, friendly school.
You would like it. But I teach religion and philosophy. Not chemistry.

In fact, until a year ago, I knew nothing about chemistry at all. I
went to a good school when I was younger, but I didn't like science.
It was hard. You had to learn a lot of material. When I was young, I
wasn't interested, and school let me drop it.

I found languages were easy and fun for me, so I did lots of
those. That meant I could give up the stuff I found difficult. Like
chemistry.

"Phew," I thought at the time. What a relief. I believed my school
was doing me a big favor. I didn't have to struggle with something tough.

But since then, I have often felt that there was something big
missing from my education.

*Hair today, gone tomorrow—
me before I understood atoms.*

Part of my job now is to watch other teachers in their classes, and to talk to them about how they teach and how to improve. Are they able to help the students understand algebra, or World War I, or how to hit a ball? How should they deal with the kid who won't listen and keeps poking his friend with a pencil?

I've seen quite a few chemistry classes, and I always felt a little embarrassed. I couldn't understand what was going on. They used language that I didn't understand. They knew how to mix substances I had never heard of.

Students sometimes asked me questions in those chemistry classes. They thought that because I was a teacher, and since this was just "basic" chemistry, I should know the answers. I could never help them, and they were a little shocked. After all, if I didn't know anything about atoms, how could I help the chemistry teacher?

I used to laugh it off. But it didn't feel good to have such a big hole in my knowledge of the universe.

Then I met Barb. This was a couple of years ago in England. She had come to share her story with my school. I found it really inspiring and relevant to me. Like me, she had been a "language person," but she realized that she could broaden her passions. She didn't allow herself to be limited to the things she liked and found easier. She told us that we could rewire our brains, which I didn't know (because I had studied so little science).

I then decided to learn high school chemistry. And I decided to do it the Barb and Terry way. I read Barb's book *A Mind for Numbers*, and I took Barb and Terry's online course, Learning How to Learn. They taught me the same tips and tricks about learning that we're teaching you in this book.

I announced to my whole school that I was going to do this. I was going to take the five-year high school chemistry exam with them that summer. And I wanted them to help me.

Normally I taught them. Now I wanted them to teach me.

The best time to plant a tree is twenty years ago.

The second best time is now.

—*Thought to be a Chinese proverb*

Students were a great help to me when I was trying to learn chemistry.

The students at my school found it funny that I was doing this. Some asked what the point was. I didn't *need* to learn chemistry for my job. I explained that I just wanted to know more about the world. And I wanted to share with them the new lessons I had learned about learning from Barb and Terry. I thought this would help them, too. And I thought it would make me a better teacher because I would remember what it was like to be a student.

My students were encouraging and amazing at helping me. They often asked me, "How's the chemistry going, Al?" as I walked around the school. The reminders would prompt me to do a Pomodoro. They recommended websites and study guides. They quizzed me on the basics. When I turned up in their chemistry classes, they would invite me to join them and their lab partners in doing experiments. And they were patient at explaining the simple things to me when I got stuck. They could have laughed at me, but they didn't. Students make great teachers.

I followed Barb and Terry's advice as much as I could. I worked in 25-minute bursts. I deliberately mixed focused sessions with diffuse breaks. Breaks usually meant walking my dog, Violet. Terry had told me how useful exercise was for him. It worked for me, too. Sometimes I explained chemistry concepts to Violet as we walked. Teaching others is a great way to learn, even if your student is a dog!

Violet sometimes had a little trouble understanding what I was explaining to her.

I would actively *recall* key information. I tested myself after each new section by working on test problems. When I didn't understand something from the book at first, I would look for videos on the internet—being careful not to get distracted. If that didn't work, I would ask one of my students. They usually knew the answer, and I knew it was good for them to teach me. It was a win-win situation.

I remembered to *interleave* by switching topics. (You'll learn more about that soon.) I looked ahead in chapters to get a sense of what was coming. I looked at old exams so I knew the kinds of things the teachers would ask. I made up zany images in my head to remember difficult material. For example, I imagined myself *crying* over a melting *white* Porsche car. This helped me to remember that the catalyst for melting aluminum is *cryolite* ("cry-a-lot"), which is a *white* powder. It worked for me . . .

I had to make sacrifices to do all this in a year, which I had promised my students I would do. I have a busy job, so I spent school vacations and some weekends studying chemistry. My family thought I was crazy. But I enjoyed getting rid of my ignorance. And I loved having a method that worked. I could feel that I was making progress.

When the exam came, I thought I would do okay, but I wasn't confident. I had done as much work as I could in one year, but most students worked on it for *five* years before taking the exam. I wished I had practiced even more. How strong were the trails on my mental pinball table?

The exam was fair. Some of it was tough, but most of it allowed me to show what I could do. When I finished, I felt like I had given it my best shot.

I had to wait eight weeks to find out my results. Like my students, I was nervous on results day. When I opened my envelope, I was really happy with it! I had passed with a good grade, and I was able to tell my students without feeling embarrassed. They shared my joy in having succeeded.

I'm really glad I did it. It allowed me to have lots of great conversations with students about learning, and I was able to share Barb and Terry's insights with them. It reminded me what it was like to be a student and to have to struggle with difficult material. Teachers often forget this because they're experts in their subjects. They sometimes don't understand why kids find things difficult. It's good to be reminded that beginners usually do find things tough! The best part was feeling like I was sharing an experience with my students. I understand their world better now, as well as understanding atoms. And I've learned some great lessons about how, together, we can become better learners.

I think a lot of adults would benefit from doing something like this. Especially those who work with young people or just spend time with them. Why don't you challenge one of your teachers to learn something new? Or your mom or dad? Offer to help them. That way you can have great conversations with them about how to be a good learner. And they will understand your world better, too.

Pause and Recall

Get up and take a little break—get a glass of water or snack, or pretend you're an electron and orbit a nearby table. As you move, see if you can recall the main ideas of this chapter.

Check this box when you're done: ❏

Now You Try! Taking a Break

Al McConville found that taking diffuse breaks between his Pomodoros helped him to learn.

Take out a sheet of paper and make a list of favorite activities that work for you when you are taking your diffuse breaks. If you'd like, ask a friend to do the same thing. Then compare your lists.

SUMMING IT UP

> **It's possible to learn new subjects that you never thought you could learn.** You can do this even when you are an adult!

> **Learning about new subjects can empower you.**

> **Use tools like the Pomodoro and active recall, and be sure to exercise** (you'll learn more about that soon!) to boost your learning.

> **Check the internet** for other explanations if the first explanation doesn't make sense to you.

> **Ask other people for help when you are stuck.**

> **Don't be afraid to go back to a beginner's level,** even if you are older than other students.

Picture walk done, a few end-of-chapter questions tackled, and notebook ready for the next chapter? ❑

CHAPTER 6

LEARNING WHILE YOU SLEEP

How to Wake Up Smarter

Wouldn't you *love* a brain upgrade? A brain "software" update? Your brain-links tightened?

Guess what? You get this upgrade every night.

Research scientist Guang Yang and the team she works with made important discoveries about learning.

The Power of Sleep

Research scientist Guang Yang* studies neurons. Guang is interested in making discoveries, like Santiago Ramón y Cajal in chapter 4. She is particularly interested in how we learn. Guang wondered whether neurons change when we learn something new. If neurons *do* change when we learn, this might give us clues about how we can learn better.

Guang found that neurons *do* change. And the big change happens after we learn something *and then go to sleep.*

Using new techniques, Guang took a picture of a living neuron. Guang's picture, below, shows part of a dendrite. You can see the dendritic spines (the "toes") that are growing out of the dendrite.

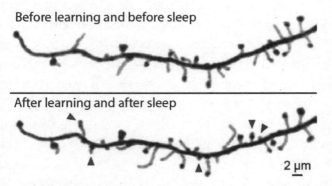

These two images show a neuron before learning and before sleep (above) and afterwards (below). The arrows on the lower picture point to new dendritic spines that grew during sleep. Notice that a few of the spines are missing. What happened to them? (Hint: See the discussion on synaptic vacuum cleaners that lies a few pages ahead!)

During the day, while the learning was taking place, a few small bumps began to emerge on the dendrite. But the spines *really* grew during sleep![1] The arrows in the above picture point to the new dendritic spines Guang found the next morning.

These dendritic spines form synapses (links) with the axons of other neurons. Wow! This means that brain-links solidify when

---

* "Guang" rhymes with "swan," and "Yang" is pronounced like "young."

you are sleeping! A neuron can even link to another neuron through *several* synapses, making even stronger brain-links.

During sleep, the brain rehearses what it has learned during the day. We can see the electrical signals traveling again and again through the same sets of neurons. It's as if, while we're sleeping, the space aliens have a chance to repeatedly pass along some friendly, reassuring shocks. Or you can imagine that during the night, your little mental mouse has a chance to run along the neural pathway many more times. This "nighttime practice" during sleep is what seems to allow the dendritic spines to get bigger.

When the dendritic spine is nice and wide, the synapse grows stronger (that is, it can send a more powerful signal). Your brain-link gets a tiny bit bigger and sturdier.

Concentrating intently during the day to learn something new can spur new dendritic "bumps" to begin to form. (This is where *active* recall comes in—it helps create those first bumps.) Then, that night while you are sleeping, the little bumps turn into dendritic spines.

The new dendritic spines have synaptic links to new neurons. As we mentioned in the earlier chapter, *the more of these links that you have, and the stronger the links are, the more powerful your sets of brain-links are.* This means that it becomes easier to think about what you are learning. It's like being able to drive your thoughts down a nice smooth road instead of a muddy alley filled with lots of potholes.

Incidentally, just reading this page of the book is helping new dendritic spines to start to form. Your brain changes when you learn!

Here's the strange thing, though. Dendritic spines are sort of like lie detectors. The new spines and their synapses only begin the growing process if you're *really* focusing on the new information you want to learn. You can't kid them. Dendritic spines can tell whether you've been playing video games or texting your friends instead of studying.

In fact, even if new dendritic spines and synapses form, they can easily fade away and disappear if you don't practice them. Use it or lose it.

It's like a "synaptic janitor" comes around and removes the dendritic spines because they're not being used. With the new imaging technology, we can watch dendritic spines disappear! Look closely at the image on the previous page and see if you can see a dendritic spine on the right that didn't make it through the night. (If you find it, give yourself a pat on the back!)

A "synaptic sweep" sweeping away dendritic spines.

That's why you can understand something your teacher tells you in class, but if you wait for a few days before reviewing the material, you may find you don't understand it at all. You then have to focus all over again on the same material. You must restart the process of growing dendritic spines just as you did the first time. Space your practice and you will remember it longer.

Now You Try! Check Your Synaptic Links

Neurons aren't only in the brain. They are also in other parts of the body. You can actually see your neurons and synapses at work. Try this experiment.

Sit on a bed and dangle your feet over the edge. Then hit your knee gently just below the kneecap. (It won't work if you don't tap just the right place.)

Be careful not to hit it too hard, but just enough to get your knee to jerk automatically. This is called a *reflex*. When you gently tap below the knee, it causes a muscle to pull above the knee. This muscle then sends a signal through a sensory neuron that travels to your spinal cord. There, the signal jumps across a synapse to a motor neuron that twitches your muscle. The strength of the synapse (that is, the strength of the signal that crosses the gap between the neurons) controls how far your knee jerks. A strong set of synapses makes your knee fly fast, but weak synapses won't move it much. This is what doctors are checking for when they tap your knee. (Don't worry if you can't make your knee jerk—some people just don't respond to the knee tap and that's still perfectly alright.)

There are many different kinds of reflexes. If someone makes a loud noise in front of your face, you will blink. If you put your fingers in a baby's palm and press, the baby will grasp them. What's cool about many reflexes is that they protect your body. When you touch a hot stove, for example, your reflexes react quickly to prevent a burn. The information only needs to travel from the muscle to the spinal cord and back, without needing to travel all the way to the brain. Traveling to the brain takes time! When your hand is on a hot stove, you want to move it as quickly as possible, and not wait to think.

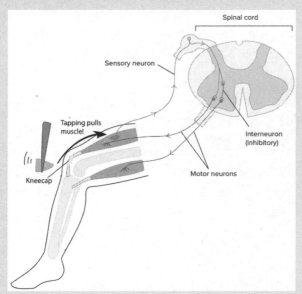

Spinal cord

Sensory neuron

Tapping pulls muscle!

Interneuron (inhibitory)

Kneecap

Motor neurons

Your doctor is checking the connections of your synapses when she gently taps below your knee. You can do this, too.

Spaced Retrieval Practice:
How to Build a Brick Wall of Learning

So, to recap: The more you learn, practice, and sleep, the more you grow new dendritic spines and synaptic links. *Stronger* links plus *more* links. Wow! What a powerful learning structure!

Good learning structures are like solid brick walls. They grow bit by bit, getting stronger all the time. If you spend some time learning a particular item each day for several days, it allows you to get several periods of sleep. This gives more time for new synaptic links to grow and helps the new learning to really take hold.[2] The neural pathway gets trampled on again and again by your mental mouse, which continues running at night, while you sleep. (Mice tend to be nighttime creatures, remember!) Practice makes permanent—or at least a lot stronger!

If you "let the mortar dry" between layers of brick by sleeping, you build a solid neural foundation. That's the wall on top. If you don't let the layers dry and cram your building (learning) into one day, the wall becomes a jumbled mess. This is also what can happen to your learning if you put everything off to the last minute.

"Cramming" means procrastinating and doing your studying at the last minute. **Now you can see why cramming is a bad idea. Leave your work to the last minute, and you have less time to repeat and fewer nights of sleep to grow new synapses—so you won't recall the details well.** There's also less time to connect your new idea to other ideas.

Some students do "reverse procrastination." If they're assigned a homework problem that's due on Friday, for example, they might do the entire homework set on Monday so it's done and out of the way. Reverse procrastination is great, but it's nice to supplement it by a little bit of review here and there before you turn the assignment in, just to give your brain a chance to strengthen the connections.

This reemphasizes the fact that when you learn something new, you want to revisit it soon—before the dendritic spines and synaptic links begin fading. If the dendritic spines and synaptic links fade away, you have to start all over in the learning process. Build on what you've already learned. Look over your notes. Explain them to a friend. Make flash cards. You can check them less often as you become better at retrieving the information.[3] Brief practice sessions over a number of days are better for storing information in memory than one long practice session.

Remember—don't just look at the answer. Pull it from your mind (the "active recall" technique), only checking the answer if you absolutely have to. This active "pulling" from your mind is what spurs the growth of new dendritic spines. *Just looking at the answer doesn't help.*

If you keep practicing each day with the new ideas,
your set of brain-links grows thicker and stronger.

Here's an example. A girl is learning some new words about the names of different parts of the brain. As you can see from the calendar on page 82, she learns the new words on Saturday—and she doesn't know them very well. She practices recalling those words on Sunday and Monday—the links start to get stronger. After three days in a row the new learning is taking hold, so she can have a day off. But the new word-links are not fixed in there yet. By Tuesday night the new learning is just beginning to fade a little. Another visit on Wednesday firms things up. One more check-in on Friday makes sure that the traces of those words in the brain are really clear. She will be in great shape for the test on Monday.

Recall is *one of the most effective ways to boost your learning.*

Another person tries to do all their learning on the Monday morning before the test. Even if they throw several hours into it, they won't have had any sleep after their learning to let the new synapses begin to form. The pathways won't begin to grow until the person goes to sleep on Monday night. Unfortunately, that's after the test—too late. The synaptic janitor soon cleans away the weak pattern. They lose!

Even worse, after cramming for a test, it's easy to think "I'm not going to use this stuff." So you don't practice with it. When you don't practice something you've only just learned, it makes it easy for your synaptic vacuum cleaners to sneak through your brain and suck away those new dendritic spines. The new links you were trying to develop end up disappearing.

There's an important idea to keep in mind here. *Some people need more practice and repetition to get a concept than others.* That's perfectly

If you don't practice with the new ideas you are learning, your synaptic sweep will sweep, and even vacuum, them away!

okay! For example, I often have to practice, practice, practice much more than other people. That's the only way I can learn the information. My coauthor Terry, on the other hand, picks up new ideas and concepts much more quickly. Our third coauthor, Al, learns some things quickly and others slowly. But even though each of us learns in different ways and at different speeds, each of us has had something good to contribute to the world of learning. So don't feel bad if it takes you longer to learn things than your friends. You can still learn the information just as well—sometimes even better!

You may have a lot of subjects you've got to study and keep on top of. That's okay. Each time you take up a subject to study, give it your *full attention* while you are studying it. Don't think about the other things you have to do. When you pick up your work for the next subject, give *it* your full attention. Having to keep up with a lot of very different topics may sometimes seem difficult, but it helps keep you mentally flexible. You can create new sets of brain-links and practice using them with lots of different subjects each day. Your brain has a galaxy of room inside—you can never even come close to filling it with new ideas and facts, no matter how hard you try!

Time to move on. In the next chapter, we're going to learn about your brain's attentional octopus!

Pause and Recall

When you are next with a family member, friend, or classmate, try this *active recall* exercise. Tell them about the most important points of what you are learning from this book or from a class you are taking. Teaching a new idea makes you think about it in new ways. Retelling allows others to become excited about learning, too. It also builds stronger brain-links in your mind, so you'll remember them better in the weeks and months to come. Even if what you are studying is complicated, simplifying so you can explain to others can build your understanding.*

Check this box when you're done: ❏

Now You Try: Repeat Your Learning After You've Slept on It

Next time you are learning something new that's a little difficult, try this experiment.

Practice several times during the first day and see if you can pull the new learning to mind after you've studied it. It's kind of hard to do, isn't it?

Now sleep on it and try a few times to pull the new ideas to mind the next day. Do you notice how much easier things start to become?

If you try for several days in a row, you'll soon notice how much easier it is to think about the new ideas. You'll be able to pull them quickly to mind when you need to.

---

* This is sometimes called the "Feynman Technique," after the brilliant and very funny physicist Richard Feynman. Here is a video by Barb's friend Scott Young (a learning adventurer!) about this technique: https://www.youtube.com/watch?v=FrNqSLPaZLc.

SUMMING IT UP

> New dendritic spines and synapses *begin* to form when you start learning new information. But **the dendritic spines and synapses really develop after your focused learning session,** while you are sleeping that night.

> **Sleep provides the "mortar" that solidifies the walls of your learning.**

> Dendritic spines and synapses develop even further when you continue to practice what you are learning. **The more you send a thought around your neural pathways, the more permanent it becomes.** That's how *sets of brain-links* are made.

> **Don't cram.** Space out your learning over several days. That way you'll have more nights of sleep for more dendritic spines and synapses to grow. Your lessons will sink in.

> **We all learn at different speeds.** Don't feel bad if someone else is quicker than you. That's life. Just put in a little more time. You'll also soon discover that being a "slow" learner can give you special advantages.

CHECK YOUR UNDERSTANDING

1. Why is sleep important when it comes to learning?

2. How are dendritic spines like lie detectors?

3. What happens to a synapse when you practice a new idea?

4. Why is it good to space out your learning?

5. Explain the "brick wall" metaphor out loud to yourself or to a friend.

6. What one thing will you do differently after reading this chapter?

(When you're done, you can compare your answers with the ones at the back of the book.)

Picture walk done, a few end-of-chapter questions tackled, and notebook ready for the next chapter? ❑

CHAPTER 7

SCHOOL BAGS, LOCKERS, AND YOUR ATTENTIONAL OCTOPUS

Imagine an attentional octopus whose arms stretch from your school bag to your locker at school.* Sound odd? Stay with me.

Your **school bag** is probably much smaller than your locker. That's good. You need to carry your school bag around. (Ever tried carrying a locker? Don't.) But there's a downside to school bags. You can't carry much in them compared to a locker.

Lockers are often bigger than school bags. They can hold a lot more stuff. There's room to decorate your locker walls and door. But a locker also has a drawback. It's not nearby. You have to walk down the hall to get to your stuff.

---

* Okay, so maybe you don't have a locker at school. Or if you do, maybe it's really small. In either case, just play along with us and pretend you have a big locker somewhere nearby that you can put your stuff in if you need to.

School bags versus lockers. Which one should you use?

Why are we talking about school bags and lockers?

You guessed it. They are metaphors. Your brain stores information like a school bag and a locker. To do this, your brain uses two different systems: **working memory** and **long-term memory**.[1]

Your working memory is like your school bag. It's small. It can't hold much. More than that, things can fall out. But it's really handy. It holds whatever you're consciously working on. That's why it's called *working* memory.

Your locker is like your long-term memory. It's in the background, down the hallway. You can store a lot more information in the locker than in the school bag. But sometimes there's so much stuff in your locker that it's hard to find what you're looking for.

Working Memory:
Introducing Your Attentional Octopus

Let's explore your mental school bag, that is, your *working memory*. Imagine that a friendly little attentional octopus lives in your mental school bag. The octopus allows you to hold ideas in your mind.

Your octopus makes a tiny little electric spark at the end of each of its arms. This helps it to "speak" to neurons.

Your attentional octopus is another metaphor. As we know, metaphors are a great way to learn.

Your attentional octopus—that is, your working memory—lives toward the front of your brain. That's in your *prefrontal cortex*. It's just above your eyes.

Your attentional octopus lives in your mental school bag—that is, your working memory. It has four arms it can use to hold the information that you are working with.

Your attentional octopus helps you to hold information in working memory. It deals with things you have in mind *right now*. You might be introduced to three people: Jon, Meg, and Sara. Your octopus uses its arms to hold those names in mind.

Wait. Was her name Sara? Or was it Sally? Your octopus's arms can be a little slippery. Information can slip out. That's why we repeat something we want to remember temporarily. Like names. "Sara, Sara, Sara." Or phone numbers. Or the list of chores your mom just told you to do. You're helping your octopus to hold on. Maybe just until you can write it down. (In fact, writing things down is one way to help the octopus hold on!)

Your attentional octopus is different from ordinary octopuses. It's electric, for one thing. And it has only four arms, so it can hold only about four things at one time. Psychologists talk about four "slots" in working memory. But I think it's a better metaphor to think of octopus arms instead.[2]

Here's an example of a mental list. "Walk dog, clean room, tease brother, do homework." Try to add any more items and you're likely to forget. Your octopus doesn't have enough arms.

When you're not focusing on something, the octopus drops the information and dozes off. It's waiting for you to wake it up and put it to work again.

If you're not focusing on something, your attentional octopus drops the information and dozes off.

How do you wake up your attentional octopus? By *focusing* on information. Ever forgotten a name right after you heard it? You weren't focusing. If the octopus is asleep, it can't grab the information.*

Mental challenges like putting together this puzzle, or doing a math problem, can make your attentional octopus really busy.

---

* Incidentally, your attentional octopus is asleep in diffuse mode. The octopus arms can still zap away randomly and make new connections, though. That's where creativity comes from!

When you learn something new, your working memory buzzes with electrical activity.[3] Your octopus is busy, arms all entangled with each other. Here's a picture of your attentional octopus when you're focused on learning something hard, such as a physics problem or a new idea in biology or translating a German sentence.

Learning something new can really put your attentional octopus to work!

Everybody has an attentional octopus. But each octopus is a little different. Most have four arms, but some can have five or even more. These can hold more information in mind. Some octopuses have only three arms. They can't hold as much information. Some octopuses have arms that can grasp firmly. Information "sticks" easily. Other octopuses have more slippery arms. Information seems to slide away.*[4] What kind of octopus do you have? Don't worry if you think yours has fewer arms. Or slippery arms. That might seem bad. But in some cases, it is very useful.

In any case, your octopus can get tired. It can hold on to information for just a little while—maybe ten to fifteen seconds. Then the information begins to slip away unless you concentrate or repeat it to hold it in mind. If you want to remember information for a long time, it needs to go somewhere else. Somewhere safer than working memory. What to do?

---

* As people get older, into their sixties and beyond, their octopus grip can loosen. But as you'll see in chapter 14, action-style video games can help tighten that grip back up again. Research has shown that video games can bring a sixty-year-old's attentional abilities back to that of a person in their twenties!

Long-Term "Locker" Memory

Fortunately, your brain has another memory system: *long-term memory*. That's like your "locker." You can store a *lot* more information in your locker. It's like something from a magician's show. Small on the outside, but huge on the inside. You can never fill it. The faces of your friends are in there, your favorite jokes, the layout of your school. And lots of facts and concepts. Anything you remember from your past is in your long-term memory. Where is your long-term memory in your brain? It's not mostly in one area like your working memory. It's much more spread out.

Each piece of information is a set of brain-links. Simple information forms small sets of brain-links. More complicated information is made up of longer, more complex sets of brain-links.

But how do you put something new into long-term memory? How do you make brain-links? Are there simple tricks to help you remember more easily?

Yes! We'll get started learning some of these tricks in the next chapter.

Pause and Recall

What were the main ideas of this chapter? Almost no one can remember a lot of details, and that's okay. You'll be surprised to see how fast your learning progresses if you tuck the main ideas into a few key sets of brain-links.

Check this box when you're done: ❏

Now You Try! Stage Your Own Memories

Remember Shakespeare's metaphor "All the world's a stage"? Make your own stage play about a school bag, a locker, and an attentional octopus! You can act out the parts in front of a mirror. Better yet, stage your play with some friends. Use this play to help explain your different memory systems, and how they work together with the attentional octopus and with brain-links to help you organize your learning.

SUMMING IT UP

> You have **two memory systems:** working memory and long-term memory.

> **Working memory** involves what you are consciously thinking about at that moment.

> The working memory system is largely in your prefrontal cortex.

> You can imagine that your working memory is like a friendly "attentional octopus" who generally has four arms. **Having only four arms explains why your working memory holds only a limited amount of information.**

> **Long-term memory** is scattered around in your brain. You have to "reach" for it with the arms of your attentional octopus. Your long-term memory has almost never-ending storage space. But you need to harness it through practice and process.

CHECK YOUR UNDERSTANDING

Check whether you've understood this chapter by answering these questions. Recalling and explaining your new knowledge strengthens it. (Remember, it doesn't help if you just look at the back of the book for the answers, instead of calling the answers up into your mind first.)

1. How is your working memory like a school bag?

2. Where in the brain does your attentional octopus "live"?

3. How many items of information can people's working memory usually hold?

4. How is your long-term memory like a locker?

5. Where in the brain is your long-term memory?

(When you're done, you can compare your answers with the ones at the back of the book.)

Picture walk done, a few end-of-chapter questions tackled, and notebook ready for the next chapter? ☐

CHAPTER 8

SLICK TRICKS TO BUILD YOUR MEMORY

Nelson Dellis was a perfectly normal kid while he was growing up. He forgot birthdays, groceries, and names. If it was forgettable, he forgot it. His dad came home one day to find a hot dog burning on the stove. Nelson had forgotten that he'd started cooking it.

But years later, at age thirty-one, Nelson found himself at the US Memory Championships. He was in the last stage of the competition. His ferocious competitors had beat him in the morning, smashing records while they rapidly memorized cards and numbers. Nelson had set a new record for names (201 names in fifteen minutes). But he was still behind. He went into the final rounds of the afternoon needing all his memory expertise to have any hope of winning. He had to memorize two decks of cards (104 cards!) in perfect order.

Could Nelson really become US Memory Champion?

Is it possible to change from an ordinary forgetful person into a memory athlete?

Nelson Dellis went from having an ordinary memory to becoming an extraordinary memory expert. How did he do it?

Looking More Deeply into
Long-Term Memory

We've already learned a lot about the octopus in your mental school bag. That is your working memory. In this chapter, we want to look more closely at what's going on in your *locker*. In other words, in your long-term memory.

Your long-term memory has two parts to it:

1. A toothpaste tube that rests on a shelf in your locker.
2. The rest of your locker.

Huh? A toothpaste tube versus the rest of the locker?

These are our metaphors for the two parts of long-term memory. Here's the key idea. Putting stuff into a toothpaste tube is *hard*. (Ever tried it?) On the other hand, it's super easy to tape a picture to the wall of a locker.

A toothpaste tube is like the "fact" part of your locker—that is, your long-term memory. It's hard to put stuff in a toothpaste tube!

Just as your attentional octopus takes information *out* of long-term memory, it also puts information *into* long-term memory. The octopus decides where to put the information based on whether it's a **fact** or a **picture**.*[1] To your brain, facts are like toothpaste. They're hard to store. So if the information is a *fact*, your octopus tries to squeeze that fact into the toothpaste tube. As you can imagine, it's a struggle! However, if the information is a *picture*, your octopus just tapes it to the wall of the locker. Done!

What do I mean by a fact? It could be something like a date. Say, the year that the silicon chip was invented, 1959.† Or the fact that the word for "duck" in Portuguese is *pato*.

These kinds of *facts* are abstract. You can't picture them very easily. This is what makes them hard to store.

Picture information is much easier to remember. How many chairs are there around your kitchen table? In your mind's eye, you can picture your kitchen table and count the chairs. You can also easily describe the route you take to the grocery store.

Here's the trick. If you convert a *fact* you are trying to remember into a *picture*, you can remember it more easily. If the picture is unusual, it's even easier to remember. And if the picture involves movement, that seems to make it stick even more strongly.

This is how Nelson does it!

Nelson's Five Tips for Remembering Things

Nelson Dellis now has a great memory because he's worked hard to develop it.‡ And he has helpful tips for how to remember virtually anything. Poems. Numbers. Speeches. Words in a foreign language. I asked Nelson for his key tips on how to get information into your head and remember it for a long time. Here's what he recommended.[2]

---

* Psychologists call these two different categories *semantic* (facts) and *episodic* (pictures).

† A silicon chip is kind of the computer's equivalent of a neuron.

‡ Nelson's book *Remember It!* is a very good one. (It's geared for adults.)

It helps to tell yourself to pay attention if you want to remember something.

1. *Focus—pay attention!* Sounds obvious, but *tell* yourself to focus. Tell yourself that what you're about to memorize is important. This helps a lot. Concentrate as much as you can on what you are working to remember. The more you practice *commanding* your focus, the better you'll get at focusing!

2. *Practice.* Nelson says, "You don't get good at something unless you practice. That's for *anything in the world.*" So practice *remembering things,* whether it's facts about biology for school, to-do lists, or the telephone numbers of your friends (you can amaze them, since almost no one does this anymore).

3. *Picture things.* Your memory is a lot better for pictures than it is for abstract facts. Turn whatever you're memorizing into a picture that you can visualize in your mind's eye. "Your brain soaks that stuff right up," says Nelson. If you add movement to your picture, it makes the image even stickier. A gorilla is one thing. A gorilla *doing the tango* is another.

4. *Store it.* Find a way to relate the information to things you already know. Find an *anchor*. This allows you to put the pictures into your brain in places where you can easily retrieve them. Even something as simple as linking a new person's name and look with someone you already know is a good anchoring strategy. (His name is *Dan*, like my uncle *Dan*, but he's way shorter.) There are other ways to store information so it's easy to grab from memory. We'll describe some of them later.

5. *Recall. Recall. Recall.* All the earlier steps in this list get information easily into your head. But this last *active recall* step, where you repeatedly bring the information to mind, is what gets it safely stored in long-term memory. You'll have to recall frequently in the beginning, but less and less often as time goes by. Flash cards are valuable here. Quizlet is a popular flash card app—it also has dictations, translations, tests, and games.

As Nelson himself says, if you have a hard time focusing, practicing memorization techniques will *improve* your ability to focus. And to memorize! Focus and memorization reinforce each other.

Here's what I mean. Let's say that Nelson has to remember three things:

1. The French word for "grapefruit" is *pamplemousse*. (The correct pronunciation is "pompla-moose.")

2. Neurons are made of *axons* and *dendrites*.

3. Eating arsenic is bad.

Nelson might come up with the following:

1. An image of a moose pumping up an inflatable grapefruit. ("Pumper-moose" should be close enough!)

2. A puzzled zombie. His ax has fallen on the floor along with

a pen. He picks them both up, straps the ax on his back, and then starts writing. Ax on, then writes (den drites)!

Ax on, then writes (den drites)!

3. A vomiting man. If you eat arsenic, you are sick!

Basically, Nelson tells himself corny visual jokes that help him remember.

You'll be amazed by how easy it is to remember things when you have a goofy way of remembering them. And it's fun making them up!

Here's an example from Al's chemistry studies. In chemistry, there's something called the "reactivity series." Basically, some chemicals blow up more easily than others. It's good to know what explodes and what doesn't! Al had to know this list for the test.

Al had to memorize these metals in the right order:

1. Potassium
2. Sodium
3. Lithium
4. Calcium
5. Magnesium

6. Aluminum
7. Zinc
8. Iron
9. Copper
10. Silver
11. Gold

That's eleven "metals" in the right order. Tough, right? You could say them over and over again, out loud, and still not remember them. So you need a trick.

Al's trick was to imagine a schoolboy in a sports uniform in a science lab. He's desperate to play a sport. The sun's shining outside. He's looking up at his teacher, who's holding a test tube. He's saying, "Please, sir, let's cancel math and zience. Instead, cricket, swimming, golf!"

The first letter of each word is the first letter of each metal. This is called a *mnemonic*. (It's pronounced "nuh-MON-ick.") Al's mnemonic allowed him to write the series down as soon as the test started. Then he could use it to solve chemistry problems. He had to rename science "zience," but it worked for him!

The Memory Palace Technique

Nelson Dellis makes crazy images in memory competitions. But he takes it a step further. To have a chance of winning, Nelson has to remember a *lot* of different wacky things. Hundreds of them. And put them in the right order.

To do this, he uses the "memory palace" technique, which uses a place you are familiar with as a memory tool. The technique has been around for 2,500 years. A famous Roman writer named Cicero used it to recall his speeches. Modern research has shown that using this technique changes your brain and helps you to start having a better memory.[3]

Imagine a place that you know well, like your house. Then take the things you need to remember and mentally "put" them in places throughout your house as you walk through it. Make sure something is shocking or silly about the way you imagine each of them. Add a little movement to them. Then picture yourself walking through the house and seeing them. Maybe even talking to them.

Let's say you need to remember some groceries. Milk, bread, and eggs.

Imagine meeting a giant milk bottle with a smiley face that smiles even more broadly when you walk through the front door.

"Hello, Mr. Milk. You're looking especially enormous today," you say.

Then in the living room, picture a loaf of bread "loafing" casually on the couch.

"Ms. Bread, you're such a *pain*. Don't you have better things to do than just lie about?" (*Pain* is French for "bread." Extra corny!)

Go through the living room into the kitchen. As you open the door, a box of eggs falls from the top of the door onto your head. Your brother is laughing at you. He set a trap. I'll let you decide what to say to him.

Your house's layout can be like a mental notepad.

Do you get the idea? The more vivid and outrageous the images, the better! You can use one memory palace for Spanish words that begin with *a*, and another for words that begin with *b*, and so forth. You can use yet another memory palace to allow you to remember the main ideas, based on a few key words, of a speech you are going to give. You can use memory palaces to remember long series of numbers, or what cards have appeared already in a card game.

The number of memory palaces you can build is immense—you can use a map of your town or country, the layout of your school, a favorite walking path, or places in your favorite video game. The memory palace technique is one of the best techniques of all to build your memory skills. Another nice thing about memory palaces is that when you're bored, like when you are waiting for a teacher, for example, you can revisit some part of a memory palace to help strengthen it. Remember, you can visit your palace from different directions—you can even revisit lists backwards!

Why Does It Work?

This ancient technique works because your brain is fantastic at remembering places and directions. It's all part of the "picture" portion of your long-term memory. Scientists call this the *visuospatial* ("VIZ-you-oh-SPAY-shell") memory. And it's supersized! Some people need a little more practice at tapping into these powers than others. But it's there.

This part of our memory is much better at remembering places and directions than it is at remembering random facts. Think of a Stone Age guy. He needed to remember how to get around. That was much more important to him than naming rocks. "That type of rock is called *quartz*? Who cares? Where's my cave?"

When was the last time you were unable to remember the way to school? Or where your living room is in your house? I'm guessing that's pretty unforgettable information. When you try to remember random things, you need to link them to things you know well. Like the route around your house. This makes them much easier to recall. As Nelson said, you also have to *focus* on the random items while you're putting them in your memory palace. It's harder at first, but you get used to it quickly.

More Memory Strategies

There are other things you can do to make difficult information more memorable:

> **Make up *songs*** about the information you want to remember. Sometimes someone else has already done it for you. If you Google "reactivity series song," for example, you will see that there are lots out there. (But don't sing them aloud during the test!)

> **Make up *metaphors*** for the information you're trying to remember. You know we love this. Think of similarities between the object or idea you want to remember and something you already know. You could try drawing it. The picture below shows how chemical bonds for benzene are like monkeys holding hands and tails.

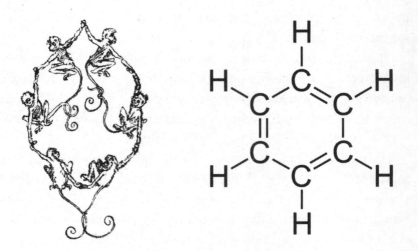

The chemical bonds for benzene are like monkeys holding hands and tails.

> **Take good notes.** We'll tell you more about this later, but handwriting (not typing) notes about the material you want to learn helps the information stick.

> **Imagine *you* are the object or idea you're trying to remember and understand.** What's it like to be a star? Or a

continent? Or a glacier? Or a tree growing in the sunlight? This might sound silly, but it works! Do some creative writing about the life cycle of an ant, or whatever you're learning.

> Some people find that **associating numbers with well-known shapes or characters** helps make the numbers more friendly and real. The number "2," for example, is shaped like a swan, while "5" curves around like a little snake. Giving personalities to numbers makes it easier to create stories that help you re-member the numbers. "52" is easier to remember because it's a snake hissing at a swan.

> **Teach the information to someone else.** Make your mom or dad or friend sit down and listen to you explain long-term and working memory. Refer to notes at first if you need to. Then try without. Practicing recall is one of the best ways of putting in-formation into your brain. And *explaining* to someone else is one of the best ways of practicing recall.

> Don't forget how important **sleep** is in anchoring these new ideas you are learning!

Quite a few of our suggestions in this chapter require you to be creative. Some of you might say, "But I'm not a creative person!" Maybe not at the moment. But as with anything, you will get better and better as you practice. Teenagers are always creative. Some-times they forget how, but they can always kick-start their creativ-ity again!

Learning Tip: The Rubber Ducky Method

A great way to learn something is to explain what you are trying to learn to an object. A rubber ducky, for example, is a really good listener. Explain what you are learning to the ducky or whatever object you choose. This can help you understand difficult and complex ideas. The rubber ducky technique is so effective that it is used by computer programmers. Line by line, they explain to the rubber duck what their code is supposed to be doing. In this way, they can discover where problems are in their code.[4]

Wrapping Up Memory

You've probably got a good sense now of some of the techniques that Nelson used to become a memory champion.

So, did Nelson win the US Memory Championship?

Yes! Not only did he win it, but he won it for the *fourth time*! Nelson says:

They were faster and better than me for sure, but in the last event (memorize two decks of cards), I went for slow and steady, making sure I memorized all 104 cards perfectly. In the end, I outlasted them. They made mistakes, and I won again.[5]

We've learned some valuable techniques in this chapter that can help you to move information into your long-term memory.

But how do you really become an expert at something?

In the next chapter, my younger daughter will give you some insight into becoming an expert. Or not. As you'll see, she had a little problem with driving a car.

Now You Try! Your First Memory List

Nelson Dellis pointed out five tips for storing something in memory. Can you create a memory palace and store Nelson's tips in your long-term memory? Think about Nelson's list, then close this book and see if you can remember it.

SUMMING IT UP

> Information is stored in memory as two types—**facts and pictures**. Pictures are much easier to remember.

> Nelson Dellis's five memory tips are:

  1. **Focus** on what you're trying to remember.

  2. **Practice** remembering.

  3. Turn what you are trying to remember into a **picture**.

  4. **Store** the picture by connecting it to things you already know.

  5. Use *active recall* to make the idea stick.

> **Memory palaces are useful,** because they use your amazing *visuospatial* powers. Practice using your memory, and it will get easier and easier.

> Five *other* ways to help you remember are to:

1. Use a **song**.

2. Make up **metaphors**.

3. **Take good notes**, preferably handwritten.

4. **Imagine** you are the thing you're trying to understand and remember.

5. **Share your ideas.** Teach them to someone else.

CHECK YOUR UNDERSTANDING

1. Is it possible to be able to develop a good memory even if you've always had a bad memory? If so, how?

2. Explain the memory palace technique.

3. Explain the differences between the two ways we store information in long-term memory.

4. Turning a fact into a picture makes the fact easier to remember. What can you do with the picture to make it stick even better in memory? Give an example.

(When you're done, you can compare your answers with the ones at the back of the book.)

Picture walk done, a few end-of-chapter questions tackled, and notebook ready for the next chapter? ☐

CHAPTER 9

WHY BRAIN-LINKS ARE IMPORTANT

(and How Not to Back a Car into a Ditch)

Here's my daughter Rachel. Notice how confused she looks. She is learning to back up a car. Backing up a car is hard! At least, at first. Should you look in the mirror, or over your shoulder, or in front of you? Too much to think about! To go the *right* way, you have to turn the wheel the *wrong* way.

Why am I telling you this? Because in this chapter, we're going

This is what my younger daughter Rachel looked like when she was first learning how to back up a car. She was very confused!

to show you that building strong brain-links is even more important than you think.[1] Why? Because brain-links help you rapidly handle complex information.

And we want to learn what happens with Rachel and the car!

Just as a reminder, a set of brain-links is made of those dendritic spine–synapse links with axons. The set of brain-links is formed in your long-term "locker" memory when you learn a concept or idea well. A nice strong set of brain-links is easy for your attentional octopus to snap onto electrically and connect into your working memory.

It's easy for your attentional octopus to snap onto a nice strong set of brain-links.

Your working memory is busy when you are first trying to figure something out. All four "arms" of your attentional octopus are juggling information. They're trying to put together the ideas, so these ideas are connected and make sense.

Your working memory is trying to create a new set of brain-links.

The creation goes in stages. First, your working memory figures out a new concept. Then you practice using the new concept. After a while, it seems natural and comfortable. That's because you've created a set of brain-links. You've made a new, nicely connected pattern in your long-term memory. Your dendritic spines and synapses have linked up, one friendly neuron reaching to the next.

It's easy for your attentional octopus to link tightly to a set of brain-links.[2] To do this, your octopus slips one of its arms out of your school bag. The arm slithers through your mental hallways, all the way into your long-term memory locker. There, it gives an electrical zap to the set of brain-links it needs. *Zap!*—a connection is formed. Suddenly, your octopus has connected the set of brain-links to your prefrontal cortex. That's your working memory. The octopus has provided a way for information stored in your locker to make it into your school bag. Now you can use the information. Easy!

Because the information is linked together beautifully, your octopus can "pull" on a brain-link packed with information. And it can pull it with just one arm.

The other three arms of working memory are free. You can think or do *other* things with those free arms. For example, you can use those free arms to grab onto other sets of brain-links. This is how you can connect complicated ideas or actions.

Your attentional octopus can easily pull up a set of brain-links that you've built with plenty of practice.

Your octopus can pull on only four sets of brain-links, but they can be linked into other sets of brain-links, so it can pull on eight, ten, or fifty sets of brain-links! This is how experts can process a lot of information and answer complex questions, even though they might have only four slots in working memory.

Your working memory (your octopus) has to work like crazy if you don't have a set of brain-links to help you do the work.

When you do have a set of brain-links, it can just sit in your long-term memory locker while your octopus relaxes, or does something different.

When your octopus needs the set of brain-links, it reaches out. As soon as it touches the links, it kicks off the electrical signal.

Through practice, you can connect links together to make longer sets of brain-links.

Experts in history, dance, chess, flying an airplane, math, or science have one thing in common. They all have lots of nice sets of brain-links, both short and long, that have nice, strong connections. And these sets of links can easily be connected with other sets of links. Experts can instantly drag huge amounts of interlinked information into the arms of their attentional octopuses!

Experts have lots and lots of sets of brain-links.

But just *understanding* a concept does not create a set of brain-links. You must *practice* a new concept to create the set of brain-links. *Understanding and practice go together.* The more you practice, the more you understand what you are learning.[3]

I should also point out that although understanding is important, there can be such a thing as *too much* emphasis on understanding.[4] Chess masters, emergency room doctors, fighter pilots, and many other experts often shut down their conscious thinking and instead rely on their well-developed library of brain-links.[5] At some point, self-consciously "understanding" why you do what you do just slows you down and interrupts flow, resulting in worse decisions or more difficulty in problem solving.

Trying to understand a concept from many different perspectives before you have it solidly linked can leave you more confused. This is especially true in areas like math. A little extra math practice with programs like Smartick and Kumon can help build stronger sets of brain-links that reinforce understanding in a deep way. Programs like these are carefully designed to allow you to gradually master each bit of knowledge before plunging ahead. This approach is called "mastery learning"—it is a great way to learn.[6]

Let's go back to my daughter Rachel. At the start of the chapter, she was learning how to back up her car. And it stressed her out! She thought she would never be able to do it. But she practiced and practiced, with plenty of feedback every time she made a mistake. Eventually, she made a beautiful "backing-up" set of brain-links. Her mental trail became deep and rich. She linked it by backing up lots of times in lots of different places. Now she can back up easily. Her "backing up the car" brain-links, along with her many other car-driving links, makes her an expert driver.

When Rachel was first trying to learn to back up, she had to focus carefully. Her attentional octopus was working as hard as it could. It used all its arms to try to process the different steps. There were no attentional arms left to hold any other information.

But now that she has created a set of links, she just thinks, "I want to back up." Her attentional octopus sends its arm slithering to the locker of her long-term memory. It sends a tiny *bzzzz* shock as it grabs on to the "backing up" brain-links. What was hard has now become easy!

Rachel can easily back up the car now. See how happy she looks!

Rachel's expertise leaves three arms in her working memory to do other things while she backs up. Like listen to music or make sure her seat belt is fastened.

Rachel is now so good at backing up that most of the time she's almost doing it in zombie mode.

That's as long as nothing out of the ordinary happens . . .

Information Overload

But what if someone tries to take her parking spot just as she's backing in? Suddenly she needs to snap out of zombie mode and think about the situation in a new way. She'll need all of her octopus arms for this. She has to stop thinking about anything else. Otherwise, she won't be able to hold on to everything. She might crash!

If your working memory has too much to handle, it's hard for you to figure things out. You get confused. (Psychologists talk about *cognitive load*.[7] Cognitive load is the amount of mental effort being used in the working memory. It's harder to move more stuff into working memory if you already have a lot going on there.)

When you're learning anything new, your working memory can only hold so much in mind at once. This is why it's so important to make strong, well-practiced sets of brain-links.

Memories Are Made of This
(Unless You're Distracted!)

So, your attentional octopus has two special quirks. It wakes up and starts to work only if you're focused. And it has only a limited number of arms.

Distraction makes things hard for your octopus. It's like putting one of its arms in a sling.

Let's say that the television is on in the background. The sound takes up some of your attention. It uses one of your octopus's arms, even if you don't think you're listening.

If you have distractions going on when you're trying to study, it's like taking away an arm of your attentional octopus.

If you're distracted, your working memory isn't able to do its job very well.[8] Your octopus has fewer arms to hold on to things. (Imagine trying to peel an orange with only one hand instead of two.)

Also, if you switch your attention, it's tiring for your octopus. It has to let go of the old information and grab the new information.

Let's say you are doing your homework. Your friend walks in and starts talking about lunch. Your octopus has to let go of some of your homework brain-links to grab on to what your friend is saying. When your friend leaves, it has to move everything back. Wow! That's tiring.

So avoid "task switching" and interruptions when you're focused on your studies.

Each time you switch your attention, you make your attentional octopus whiz its arms back and forth between different sets of links. It is tiring!

If you're lucky (or unlucky) enough to have one, think about your smartphone. Do you check it while you're hanging out with friends or family? Once you switch attention to your smartphone, you've dropped your focus from those you're with. It takes time for you to get back into the conversation. I'll bet that you notice that sometimes.

It's the same with learning. If you're doing a difficult homework problem, and you stop to look at your phone in the middle of a problem, it's like you've dropped all your brain-links. When you come back to the problem, you have to pick them up again. Your poor old attentional octopus finds this really tiring.

Enjoyment Comes with Mastery

When you are first learning something new, before you begin to create brain-links, it can often seem difficult and unenjoyable.

Let's take learning to ride a bicycle, for example. At first it was hard just to remain upright. You crashed to the ground, and sometimes it hurt. Once you began to ride upright, then you had to learn how to not press the brakes too hard, and how to turn without falling.

But once the initial, more difficult learning stage passed, you could just jump on the bike and ride. You became an expert. *Fantastic!*

This brings us to an important point. Sometimes you do not enjoy things because you have not yet mastered them. You're still in the "how do I balance my bike?" early stages, where it all can seem very difficult.

Just start! The first steps are often the most difficult. Enjoy the process and wait for the results to come.[9]

Key Ideas

Let's review the key ideas of this chapter.

Creating sets of brain-links helps you think complicated thoughts. You can easily pull up lots of interlinked information. Without sets of brain-links, your mind can become overwhelmed. Like when Rachel was first trying to back up the car.

When you're trying to learn something new, you haven't yet created brain-links. Your attentional octopus has to use all four arms. It has to work hard!

When you haven't linked the material, you can feel confused. Like you just can't *grasp* it. Of course that's not true at all. You just need to start by building some little sets of brain-links. With practice, little brain-links become longer ones. Your octopus can pull them right up and work easily with them.

The earliest steps of learning something new are often the hardest. Make a library of sets of brain-links, and you'll be well on your way to becoming an expert.

In the next chapter, you'll get to know more about Terry Sejnowski. He's a neuroscience expert. You'll find that he wasn't *always* that way, though!

Pause and Recall

What were the main ideas of this chapter? Can you picture some of these ideas with images (like the octopus) in your mind's eye? Close the book and look away as you do this. If you're having trouble, try writing the ideas down.

Check this box when you're done: ❏

Now You Try! Going Without Your Smartphone

If you have a smartphone, leave it somewhere else the next time you are doing your homework. Commit to leaving it there until your Pomodoro is over. Otherwise, you might be tempted to sneak a peek when things get tough. And that just makes it tougher to tune back in!

SUMMING IT UP

> **A set of brain-links is a pathway of connected neurons in your long-term "locker" memory that is built through practice. A set of brain-links helps your working memory to process information more quickly.** Brain-links like these are easy for your attentional octopus to grab on to.

> Your octopus gets tired if it has to keep switching its focus from one set of brain-links to a completely different one. **So try to avoid distraction and task switching.**

> Without sets of brain-links, we get confused when we try to put too much into our mental school bag. **We all have a maximum *cognitive load*.** There is a limit to what we can deal with at one time in our working memory.

> **The earliest steps of learning something new are often the hardest.** Be patient and keep working away. Look for that click of delightful enjoyment as a set of brain-links begins to form and you "get" how to do something.

CHECK YOUR UNDERSTANDING

1. Why are brain-links important?

2. Explain what your attentional octopus does.

3. A good example of a "linked" idea is tying your shoes. When you first were learning to tie your shoes, you had to pay close attention. But now you can easily tie your shoes while you talk to others, watch television, or sing a song. Name another activity or concept you have linked.

4. What happens to your attentional octopus if you work with the television on?

5. Why should you avoid "task switching"?

6. What should you do with your phone when you're working on homework? Why?

7. Does understanding a concept create a set of brain-links?

8. How do you get to be an expert at something?

9. If you were to be rescued from a burning building, would you choose a firefighter who had just watched people being rescued from burning buildings? Or would you choose a firefighter who had physically practiced rescuing people from burning buildings? Why?

(When you're done, you can compare your answers with the ones at the back of the book.)

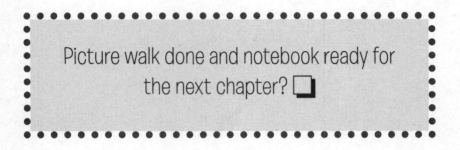

Picture walk done and notebook ready for the next chapter? ☐

CHAPTER 10

LEARNING WITH CLUBS AND GROUPS, FINDING YOUR MISSION, AND HOW TERRY NEARLY BURNED DOWN THE SCHOOL

Hi, my name's Terry Sejnowski.* Great to meet you!

I was different from Barb and Al growing up. I was the "science guy" in elementary school, but I didn't get along with languages. I had a chemistry lab in my basement. I loved making bright flashes, bangs, and clouds of smoke. When I was seven years old, I made a papier-mâché volcano that set the smoke alarm off. Everyone in the school had to evacuate. They all remember the day I nearly burned down the school!

---

* My last name's pronounced "say-NOW-ski."

Terry the Troublemaker

In high school, I was bored in my science classes. They were too simple for me because I had gotten ahead. I asked a lot of questions, but I was told that I was disrupting the class. I was a "troublemaker." (Mind you, just because you're bored doesn't mean that the work's too easy for you. It might just mean you aren't being curious enough!)

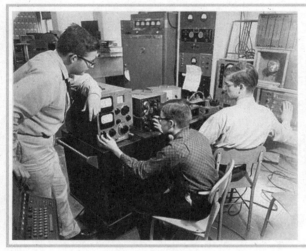

My fellow club members and I are preparing to bounce radio signals off the moon in the Radio Club at St. Joseph High School in Cleveland. I'm the one in the middle.

Radio club saved me. We were a group of science lovers who used to meet after school to learn about and build radios. We practiced sending signals using Morse code. We even bounced radio signals off the moon using antennas we'd built. Finally, I could ask whatever questions I liked!

One of the best ways to have satisfying experiences at school is to join clubs and groups at your school that do activities you enjoy. (If you are homeschooling, there are often ways to join clubs and groups outside of or even connected to local schools.) Don't be afraid to ask about forming a new club if it doesn't exist at your school (like a Learning How to Learn club!). Finding friends with whom you can share what you love doing is an excellent way to develop true friendships and help your creativity bloom.

The club members and I are adjusting a radio antenna on the roof of my high school. (I'm the one on the left.)

What Is Your Mission?

One day the teacher supervising the radio club asked me a question: "What is your mission?"

I didn't know, but it made me start to think about the future. I needed to grow up and find something to do in life. I was most interested in gravity and brains. How does gravity travel? Why can my brain learn some things really quickly (like physics) and not other things (like languages)?

I wish I knew then what I now know about the brain and how to learn. I would have done much better at languages, like Barb and Al. I had taken classes in German. But it wasn't until later when I had a German girlfriend that I learned enough German to at least get by. Maybe I just wasn't motivated enough in high school.

What I Learned at Princeton

I was lucky, and my career in science went well. I received some wise advice from a famous professor, Carl Anderson. Like Santiago Ramón y Cajal, Carl Anderson had won a Nobel Prize. (He discovered the positron.*) Professor Anderson asked me if I wanted to do theory or experiment. I said: "Why not both?" He said it was possible and gave an example of someone at Caltech, who I later got to know.

Getting advice from someone you respect can have a big impact on your life.

---

* The *positron* ("PAWZ-ih-tron") is like a positive version of an electron.

I learned a lot of physics in graduate school at Princeton University.* I made exciting discoveries about black holes and gravity. I was lucky to have good mentors and smart friends. **It really helps to work on difficult problems with other people. Find people who let you sparkle. Hanging around with people who have good ideas can boost good ideas of your own!**

I had reached a turning point. I had answered my questions about physics and gravity. But I still didn't know much about the brain. Yogi Berra, the philosopher-catcher of the New York Yankees baseball team, said something wise: "When you come to a fork in the road, take it." I took the road to biology.

Here I am at Princeton. Black holes competed with brains and other interests for my attention. Brains won.

Jumping into the Brain

The mysteries of the brain are as complex as the mysteries of outer space. Like Barb and Al, I had to go back to the basics. It was tough at first because others already knew so much. But I found that my training in physics helped me think about biology in ways that

---

* Graduate school is the more advanced part of university studies. Usually the first three to five years of university studies allow you to get an "undergraduate" degree. Then after that, some people continue on at the university and do more advanced "graduate" studies in graduate school.

others couldn't. It's amazing how subjects connect in ways that you don't expect!

I had read about neurons in books. However, they only became real to me during a summer course at Woods Hole in Massachusetts, where I got to see them under a microscope. There's an important lesson here. Learning comes to life when you *do* something with information. Make it active. Don't just read it. I recorded electrical signals from many different types of neurons. What I had learned at my high school radio club about radio signals really helped. (You never know when your knowledge is going to come in handy.)

Artificial Brains

In my job, I use my knowledge of physics and biology to compare brains with computers. In some ways, they're similar—in other ways, they're really different. Computers are unbelievably fast at doing calculations. They are incredible at doing one thing after another at lightning speed.

This is me today at the Salk Institute in La Jolla, California. The Salk Institute is one of the best institutes in the world for research on neuroscience and medicine.

Brains are different. They're much slower, and they work by doing lots of smaller things all at once. They're like a team of billions of tiny computers working together. Each neuron is a tiny "computer." As you know from the earlier chapters, each neuron-computer is connected to the other tiny computers by synapses.

This teamwork allows brains to do things that computers find really hard, like seeing and hearing.

There's something for all of us to learn about how amazing our brains are. By working closely with other people, and spending a lot of time thinking about how the brain works, I have found ways to make "artificial brains." These are electronic, not the sort you have in your head. These computers learn like brains and have to go to school like you (sort of). They have a new kind of artificial intelligence—"AI"—that never gets tired or bored. I expect you will hear more about AI in the near future. Science fiction is coming true!

Neuroscientists have made astonishing progress in the last thirty years. We used to know hardly anything about how the brain works. Now we know a lot more, including plenty of things about how the brain learns. For example, we know the important effects of exercise and sleep on making stronger memories. I have made exercise an important part of my daily life. I know it helps me think and learn much better. You'll learn much more about exercise in the next chapter.

Happy learning!

Pause and Recall

What were the main ideas of this chapter? You will find that you can recall these ideas more easily if you relate them to your own life and career goals. Close the book and look away as you try this.

Check this box when you're done: ❏

SUMMING IT UP

> **Find something that really grabs your interest at school.** Find your own version of radio club.

> **Don't be afraid to ask.** If your school doesn't have activities that interest you, ask them to set something up. Or you can start a club yourself with some help from the school.

> **Be ready to work with others.** Hang out with creative people and see how many more ideas you start to have yourself.

> **Make your learning active whenever you can.** Put things you learn from books into practice, as well as reading about them.

> **Be amazed by your brain!** It's as if you have billions of tiny computers all working together for you.

> **Learning in one area can give you more ideas in other areas.** Subjects connect. Physics can help with biology. And it might even help with art, sports, or making friends!

Picture walk done, a few end-of-chapter questions tackled, and notebook ready for the next chapter? ☐

CHAPTER 11

HOW TO PUMP UP
YOUR BRAIN

In 2015, Julius Yego became the World Javelin Champion. He threw his javelin 92.72 meters. He threw it so hard he fell over! He soon got up to celebrate, though.

Julius has an extraordinary story. He grew up in a poor part of Kenya, in what is known as Africa's Rift Valley. When he became interested in the javelin, he had to make his own spears. He made them out of branches from trees. In Kenya, the most popular sport is running. There weren't proper javelins. There was no javelin coach in the whole country, and Julius didn't even have the right shoes. But he was determined. Julius got better and better each year until he was world champion. How did someone with no coach and little support beat athletes from countries where they spend a fortune on sports? I'll tell you soon.

Julius Yego became a world champion javelin thrower. He learned to throw the javelin in a very unusual way.

Of course, part of Julius's success had to do with the fact that he exercised a lot. That's what this chapter is about. What does exercise have to do with learning? A lot, as it turns out, and not just for learning how to throw javelins.

Exercise Pumps Up Your Brain!

One part of your brain is particularly important for remembering facts and events. It's called the *hippocampus.** You can see what the hippocampus looks like below.

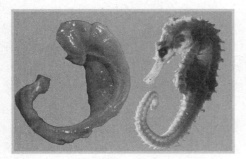

Hippocampus (left) means "sea horse" (right) in Greek. Do you see the resemblance?

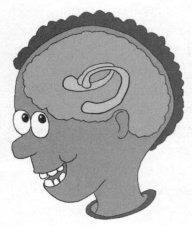

If you flip the hippocampus upside down, you can see how it fits into the brain. Technically, the brain has two hippocampi—one on the left and the other on the right side of the brain.

---

* We can't resist. What did the hippocampus say during its retirement speech? "Thanks for the memories."

Interestingly, during sleep, information you've learned is transferred from the neurons in the hippocampus into the neurons of your *cerebral cortex*, which is the outer layer of the brain. Your cerebral cortex is the home of your long-term memory (locker). **So sleep not only helps build new synaptic connections, it also clears out the hippocampus to make room for new learning.**

Some unfortunate people who have damage to the hippocampus suffer from amnesia—they can't remember anything that happens to them after a few minutes. Interestingly, they can still remember what they learned before the damage. That is, they can still remember the earlier memories that sleep had cemented in their cerebral cortex.

All this means that the hippocampus is a key player when it comes to memory. New neurons are born in the hippocampus every day. It's like a high school basketball team. New players arrive every year, while the older ones leave. The new players are often busy learning new plays.

If you don't learn anything new, the new neurons in your hippocampus will disappear not long after they are born. (In a similar way, a new basketball player tends to disappear from the team if he or she doesn't bother to learn new plays.) If you have new learning experiences, however, the new neurons will stay on and allow you to remember. New synapses from both older neurons and new neurons in the hippocampus make new sets of brain-links. When you sleep, these new brain-links in the hippocampus help make the brain-links in the long-term memory of the cerebral cortex stronger.*

Over twenty years ago, my coauthor Terry helped make an amazing discovery about new neurons.[1] *Exercise helps new neurons grow.*

When you exercise, your brain makes a chemical called BDNF.[2] That's short for "Brains Definitely Need Food!" (Al, my other coauthor, made that up. It might help you remember. "BDNF" is really short for "brain-derived neurotrophic factor." But that's less snappy.)

---

* Technically, this firming up of information as it moves from the hippocampus into the cerebral cortex is called "memory consolidation."

BDNF makes your new neurons strong and healthy.[3] It protects them from injury and makes them more likely to connect to other neurons. It also acts like a food for synapses and dendritic spines, making them grow larger. You can see how the dendritic spines have grown larger in the picture below.

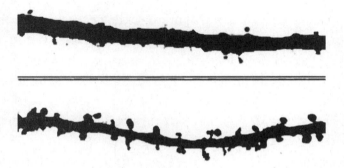

The upper image is a dendrite in the hippocampus that hasn't been exposed to BDNF. Notice that there are barely any dendritic spines ("toes"). The lower image shows what happens after BDNF is applied. Wow! The dendritic spines grow tall and broad! These spines make it easy to connect through the synapses to other neurons. If you exercise regularly, your neurons are going to look more like the bottom version, able to connect and chat with a lot of other neurons!

Just like fertilizer helps plants grow, BDNF helps neurons grow. Extra BDNF is produced by exercise.

So when you exercise, you're looking after your brain, and obviously your body, too!

Food *Also* Feeds Your Brain!

You may be wondering whether what you eat affects how you learn. The answer is, yes, it does! In fact, if you exercise *and* have a healthy diet, it has a big impact on your ability to learn and remember. Bigger than either exercise or healthy eating alone.[4]

So what does it mean to eat healthily? Research shows that adding fruits and vegetables to your diet is a good idea. Try for a variety. Vegetables from the **onion** family, which includes garlic and leeks, contain chemicals that help keep away all sorts of diseases, from diabetes to cancer. So do vegetables from the **cabbage** family, which includes cauliflower, broccoli, radishes, and Brussels sprouts. Fruits of all colors are also great, including oranges, pears, blueberries, cherries, and raspberries. **Dark chocolate** has some of the same good-for-you chemicals as fruits, and more besides. (But choose chocolate with low sugar, and avoid eating chocolate later in the day, as it can interfere with your sleep.) **Nuts** are also chockfull of healthiness. A handful of nuts a day can nicely round out your diet.

Try to avoid "fake foods" that have had most of the nutrition processed out of them. The "fake food family" includes foods like French fries, chips, chicken nuggets, and anything with a lot of sugar or white flour in it, like doughnuts, some breakfast cereals, and soft drinks. Dessert is not a food group.

Everyone has different ideas about the healthiest diet to follow. A Mediterranean-style diet is a good choice. As you might guess, it's a diet that grew up around Mediterranean countries like Greece, Italy, Portugal, and Spain. It has lots of fruits, vegetables, fish, olive oil, and whole grains.

You Can Learn from Many Sources!

Back to Julius Yego. How did he keep improving? He didn't have a coach or all the advantages of a richer country: sports scientists, psychologists, and nutritionists.

Here's the surprising thing about Julius. He became a champion by watching lots of YouTube videos of javelin throwing and then trying it himself. He sat in a cybercafé (a place where he could access the internet) for hours studying his heroes. And then he practiced a lot out in the African hills. In the end, he did get a coach from another country. But for a long time, all of his coaching came from the internet. He later became known as Mr. YouTube Man!

Why am I telling you this story? Well, it's an inspiring story. But it also brings together the two important areas in this chapter. *Exercise* and *learning*. I also want to show you that you don't necessarily need to learn from a book or a teacher. You can teach yourself by using the internet and other resources. And by practicing, practicing, and even more practicing, getting feedback however you can.

So, Julius Yego must be a genius as well as a champion athlete, right? Well, he might be. I don't know him personally. But his brain is in much better shape than if he had just watched YouTube videos. He watched *and* he practiced. He learned new information, and he practiced it! That's the goal for you, too.

I think Terry *is* a genius. I know he makes exercise a really important part of his day. He loves to jog by the ocean. For him, it's a great way of slipping into diffuse mode. It's often when he's out jogging that he comes up with his best ideas. He's exercising because he likes it *and* because it's good for his brain. But also because the new ideas help him with his job as a professor.

Exercise:
An All-Purpose Tool for Good Health

Exercise does something else magical. It enables your brain to produce other chemicals, such as serotonin and dopamine.[5] These chemicals help you come up with new ideas. They allow you to see how old ideas can link up to form new ones. Then you can think in new ways. All those little thought-mice running about are sure to find new perspectives on the forest.

Exercise isn't just good for every organ in your body. It's good for your brain, too. It improves understanding, decision-making, and focusing. It assists with remembering and switching between tasks. It can also help people recover from mental illness. Some psychiatrists say that exercise is stronger than any medicine.

Pause and Recall

Sometimes you feel featherbrained as you're trying to look away and recall a key idea. Or you find yourself reading the same paragraphs over and over again. When this happens, do something physical—for example, a few sit-ups, push-ups, jumping jacks, or cartwheels. These can have a surprisingly positive effect on your ability to understand and recall. Try doing something active now, before recalling the ideas of this chapter.

Check this box when you're done: ❑

Now You Try! Exercise!

So what are you waiting for? Are you still sitting down reading this book? Get out there and chase a mouse! Wrestle a zombie. Vacuum a stair. Tickle an octopus. Carry a locker. Whatever exercise you like. Enjoy your diffuse mode! (But remember to come back later and finish the book.)

SUMMING IT UP

> **You can learn from the internet, as well as from teachers and books.**

> **Exercise is really good for your neurons,** especially the new ones.

> Exercise helps create a chemical (BDNF) that is like **food for your brain.**

> **Exercise releases chemicals that generate new ideas.**

> **Exercise is a great diffuse activity!**

CHECK YOUR UNDERSTANDING

1. What part of your brain is particularly important for remembering facts and events? (Hint: It means "sea-horse" in Greek, and it looks like one.)

2. How is your brain like a high school basketball team?

3. When BDNF is added to the brain, the _____ _____ grow tall and broad.

4. Describe five ways exercise is healthy for you.

5. What are some elements of a healthy diet?

(When you're done, you can compare your answers with the ones at the back of the book.)

Picture walk done, a few end-of-chapter questions tackled, and notebook ready for the next chapter? ☐

CHAPTER 12

MAKING BRAIN-LINKS

How Not to Learn from a Comic Book

When I was a kid, I was a little sneaky.

My parents wanted me to play the piano, and I wasn't that excited about it. But I did as they asked. Kind of.

Every week, my teacher gave me a new song to practice. I would also practice older songs that I'd already learned. It was a lot easier and more fun to practice the older songs!

My parents could hear the piano going in the background, but they never paid attention to what I was playing.

I'd spend five minutes practicing the new song. Then I would put a comic book on the music stand in front of me. I would play the older song over and over again for twenty-five minutes while I read the comic book. Altogether, this made a half hour of practice.

Was I improving my ability to play the piano? Or was I just kidding myself? And what did my parents do when they realized what I had done?

Becoming an Expert

Let's step back and remind ourselves about brain-links.

A set of brain-links is a well-practiced thought-trail. (Remember, we can also think of them as wide, smooth mouse pathways in the forest.) Your attentional octopus can easily reach out and link to the right brain-links whenever it needs a little help with its thinking—that is, if you have taken the time to build them. Having lots of brain-links relating to a topic is key to becoming an expert.*

See the puzzle on the top of the next page? Every time you create a solid set of brain-links, it's like connecting some pieces of a puzzle. When you've created enough links, the puzzle starts filling in. You begin to see the big picture of the subject. Even if there are a few small link-pieces you haven't filled in, you can still see what's going on. You have become an expert!

But what if you *don't practice* with your newly developing brain-links? You can see what happens then by looking at the faded puzzle at the bottom of the page. It's like trying to put together a washed-out puzzle. It's not easy.

---

* Remember, having a lot of brain-links isn't the same as just memorizing a bunch of facts. William Thurston, who won the Fields Medal (that's the top prize in mathematics), probably put it best when he said, "Mathematics is amazingly compressible: you may struggle a long time, step by step, to work through the same process or idea from several approaches. But once you really understand it and have the mental perspective to see it as a whole, there is often a tremendous mental compression. You can file it away, recall it quickly and completely when you need it, and use it as just one step in some other mental process. The insight that goes with this compression is one of the real joys of mathematics." Thurston was talking about the power of a beautiful, well-built set of brain-links.

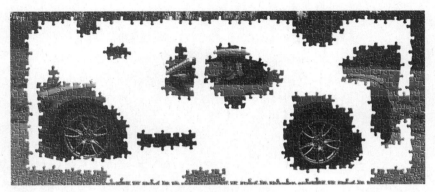

Each time you create a set of brain-links, you are fitting together pieces of a puzzle. The more you work with your links, the more you see how they fit in with other links. This creates bigger sets of links.

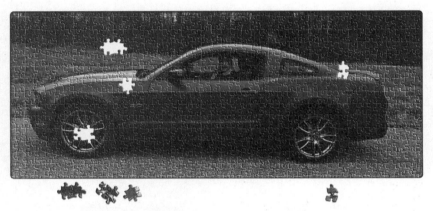

When you've built and practiced with enough links, you see the big picture! You've become an expert.

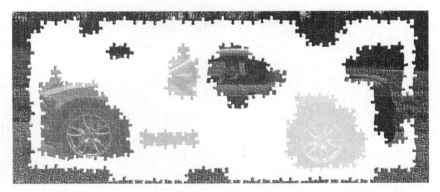

If you don't practice with your links, they start to fade. This makes it harder to see the pieces, which makes the puzzle harder to put together.

Two Key Ideas Behind Linking

This brings us to a critical question. *How do you go about making a set of brain-links?* Two key ideas will help get you started—one involves practice and the other, flexibility.

1. Deliberate Practice (Versus Lazy Learning)

When you practice enough, you can build solid brain-links. But the way you practice is important. When you've got an idea well linked, it's easy to practice, and it feels good. But this can turn into "lazy learning." Lazy learning doesn't encourage new daytime "bumps" on your dendrites that can turn into solid new neural connections while you sleep. When you can read comic books while you're practicing, it's time to move on.

The best way to speed your learning is to avoid lazy learning. If you spend too much time on material you already know, you won't have time to learn *new* material.

This idea of focusing on the harder stuff is called *deliberate practice.*[2] Deliberate practice is how you become an expert more quickly in whatever you are studying.[3]

2. Interleaving (or How to Teach Interstellar Friends)

Developing flexibility in your learning is also important. Here's a story to demonstrate this: Let's say that you make a new friend, named "Leaf," from an exotic planet where they use advanced technologies. Your new friend has never used hammers or screwdrivers before.

You want to teach Leaf how to use a hammer and a screwdriver. Because you know about cognitive load,* you're careful not to teach Leaf too much at once.

You start by showing Leaf how to use a hammer. He learns to pound in lots of nails. After a couple of hours of practice (Leaf is a clumsy interstellar friend), he's got the idea of how to nail, well, *nailed.*

Next, you give Leaf a screw. To your surprise, Leaf starts trying to hammer the screw into a board.

Why? Because *when the only thing Leaf has used is a hammer, everything looks like a nail.* Leaf is applying the wrong technique to solve the problem, because he hasn't studied and practiced *when* he should use one of the two different techniques.

It's important not just to practice a given technique or item. It's also important to practice *choosing between techniques or items.* This is true when you're learning all sorts of topics.

Practicing different aspects and techniques of the skill you are trying to learn is called *interleaving.*[4] (Just remember your *interstel*lar friend, *Leaf.* Interleave—get it?)

Here are some visuals to help you better understand the idea of interleaving. When you study a typical topic you are learning in class, say "Topic 7," you are often assigned a batch of homework

---

* Remember, cognitive load is the amount of mental effort being made in the working memory.

problems related to Topic 7.* Here's an example (the problem numbers refer to problems that your teacher assigns from a textbook):

Plain Assignment

Topic 7 problem 4
Topic 7 problem 9
Topic 7 problem 15
Topic 7 problem 17
Topic 7 problem 22

But when you interleave, you start mixing in other types of problems, so you can see the difference. Notice below how the shaded boxes cover different topics that are mixed into the Topic 7 problems. In that way, you can become comfortable not only with Topic 7, but also with the differences between Topic 7 and Topics 4, 5, and 6.

Interleaved Assignment

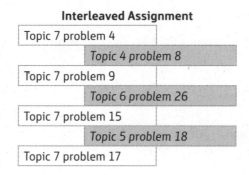

When you interleave with different topics, you can almost feel your brain go, *Wait a minute, what's this? I didn't expect to go back to that*

---

* Educators sometimes call a noninterleaved assignment a "blocked" assignment, because the subject is worked on all in one block.

Incidentally, *interleaving* is good because it allows your attentional octopus to consciously compare different techniques. This helps you develop new "deciding" links that allow you to figure out which techniques to choose. *Task switching*, on the other hand, is bad because you're just dragging your attentional octopus from topic to topic. This makes your octopus do unnecessary work every time you switch tasks.

Interleaving is often difficult for textbook writers to do. This is because there is a natural need for questions at the end of each chapter that focus on that chapter. This means that interleaving is up to you, the reader!

other stuff! But then you'll notice how you begin to see differences between the topics in ways you hadn't previously imagined.

Making a Set of Brain-Links

Now we can finally explain some of the best ways to make sets of brain-links in different subjects.

Focus

The most important step is the first one: focus. Memory champion Nelson Dellis told us that focusing is important for memorizing. But focus is also important more generally, for any information you want to link. You've got to use all the arms of your attentional octopus. No TV. No phone. You're going to be forming some new brain-links, so you need to concentrate. Maybe grab your Pomodoro timer. Tell yourself: *This is important—I need to focus!*

(*Psst!* Can you make new brain-links if you're *not* paying close attention? Maybe. If it's super-easy material. But it'll take you a *lot* longer to make the links.)

Do It—Active Practice!

If the brain-links you're creating involve a physical action, then *focus* and *do it*. For example, if you're learning how to score a basket in basketball, you need to practice making a basket. And then you need to do it again, perhaps from a different angle. Again. And again. And again. You'll be getting constant feedback, because if you're doing it wrong, you won't make a basket. Likewise, if you're learning a language, you'll need to *listen* and *say* the words over and over, and if possible, get feedback from a native speaker. If you're learning to play a musical instrument, you'll need to practice new tunes. Or if you're learning to draw, you'll need to try different techniques. Get feedback from teachers wherever you can to correct yourself.

The key is to actively practice or bring to life whatever you are learning *yourself.* Just watching other people, or looking at a solution, or reading a page, can allow you to get started. But it won't do much to build your own neural structures of learning. Remember Julius Yego with the javelin. He wasn't just passively *watching* YouTube. He was focusing on the techniques and then *actively practicing* them.[5]

Practice your new skill over a number of days, making sure you get some good sleep each night. This helps your new synaptic brain-links to form. You want to broaden the forest pathways—thicken the links—for your mental mouse.

You also need to "change up" what you are doing. In soccer, you need to learn to dribble the ball, cross, pass, or shoot it. And you need to be able to tackle and chip the ball, too. It's not just about kicking the ball any old way! All these skills are separate, but related. To

become a soccer expert, each skill needs to be practiced separately during training, then interleaved. You want your reactions to become automatic during the heat of a match.

Whether you are learning martial arts, dance, an additional language, knitting, welding, origami, gymnastics, or the guitar, it's all the same. *Deliberate practice with interleaving.* Focus on the hard stuff and mix it up. That's how you become an expert.

Special Advice for Math, Science, and Other Abstract Subjects

Let's say you're trying to make a set of brain-links in math or science. See if you can work a problem by yourself. *Show your work and write your answer out with a pencil.* Don't just look at the solution and say, "Sure, I knew that . . ."

Did you have to peek at the solution to get a little help? If so, that's okay, but you'll need to focus on what you missed or didn't understand.

Next, see if you can work the problem again, without looking at the solution. And again. Do this over several days.

Try not to peek at the solution!

At first, the problem may seem so difficult that you could *never* work it! But it will eventually seem so easy that you will wonder how you could have thought it was hard. Eventually, you won't even have to write the solution out with a pencil. When you just look at the problem and think about it, the solution will flow swiftly through your mind, like a song. You've created a good set of brain-links.[6]

Notice something important here. You've used *active recall* to help you create your brain-links. As we mentioned earlier, active recall is one of the most powerful techniques there is to boost your learning.

A key idea here is that you are not blindly memorizing solutions. You are looking at problems and learning how to build your own brain-links. Once that solid, beautiful set of links is formed, it can easily be pulled up into working memory when you need to. With enough practice independently solving the problem (*not* looking at the solution!), each step in the solution will whisper the next step to you.*

---

* Occasional memorization, such as the multiplication tables, can be helpful. This is because your brain naturally begins to analyze the patterns and relationships it sees as you embed the tables in your brain. The embedding process helps you to get a naturally better feel for the numbers and how they relate to one another. But as always, it's never a good idea to just memorize without having an understanding of what you're doing. (It's like memorizing a word in a foreign language without understanding what it means. How would you ever be able to use it later on?) And the more you practice using a variety of problems, the deeper and richer your feel for the numbers will become.

A big reason for my bad math grades when I was a
teenager was that I looked at the answers in the back
of the book. I fooled myself that I already knew how to
get those answers. Boy, was I wrong! Now, as an adult,
I'm having to re-learn math. But at least now
I know not to fool myself!

—Richard Seidel

Special Advice to Improve Your Writing

The techniques we described to improve your math and science skills are very similar to what you can do to improve your writing!

Famous statesman Benjamin Franklin was a terrible writer when he was a teenager. He decided to do something about his problem. He took pieces of excellent writing and jotted down a word or two of the key idea of some of the sentences. Then he tried to re-create the sentences from his head, just using the key ideas as hints. By checking his sentences against the originals, he could see how the originals were better—they had a richer vocabulary and used better prose. Benjamin would practice this technique again and again. He gradually began to find that he could improve on the originals!

Famous American statesman Benjamin Franklin was a lousy writer as a teenager. He decided to change himself by actively developing his writing links.

As Benjamin's writing improved, he challenged himself to write poetry from the hints. Then he began scrambling the hints, to teach himself about how to develop a good order in his writing.

Notice—Benjamin wasn't just sitting around memorizing other people's good writing. He was *actively building writing links*, so he could more easily pull good writing from his mind.

Can you think of how you might do something similar if you want to improve your artistic ability?

Back to the Piano

So, was I learning the piano well when I was reading the comic book? Not at all! I broke just about every rule of good learning. I wasn't deliberately focusing on the new and harder material. Instead, I was using lazy learning, mostly only playing songs I already knew well. Sure, I slept on my new learning, but with only five minutes of real study a day on new information, it was no wonder I didn't make much progress. I wasn't learning enough new material to be able to interleave anything. Gradually, because I wasn't getting better quickly, I lost what little interest I had. My parents never realized the trick I played on them—and on myself. Today, sad to say, I can't play the piano at all. This is a double shame because research is showing that learning a musical instrument is healthy for your brain in many ways. It can help you learn countless other skills more easily.

Lady Luck Favors the One Who Tries

You may say, "But, Barb, there's so much to learn! How can I ever make brain-links out of it all when I'm trying to learn something new, abstract, and difficult?"

The short answer is, you can't learn it all. Your best approach is to pick some key concepts to turn into brain-links. Link them up well.

Remember what I like to call **the Law of Serendipity: Lady Luck favors the one who tries.**

Just focus on whatever section you are studying. Follow your intuition on the most important information to link. You'll find that once you put the first problem or concept in your library of brain-links, *whatever it is*, then the second concept will go in a bit more easily. And the third more easily still. Not that all of this is a snap, but it does get easier.

Good fortune will smile upon you for your effort.

Lady Luck favors the one who tries.

Pause and Recall

What were the main ideas of this chapter? Remember to congratulate yourself for having finished reading this section—every accomplishment deserves a mental pat on the back! Close the book and look away as you try this.

Check this box when you're done: ❏

Now You Try! Brain-Link to Mastery[7]

> Choose a subject you really want to improve in. Think about what skills or knowledge you should deliberately practice so that you can move ahead. Identify specific tasks you can

perform. Be clear about what would signal the level of mastery that should lead to your dropping that task in order to deliberately practice further, more complex tasks.

> Cut colored construction paper into strips to make a set of paper brain-links. Each strip will be a loop in the set of links. You can use colors to indicate categories or types of tasks if you'd like, or just alternate colors in a fun pattern.

> Write down one task on each of the paper strips. Then make the paper strips into links. Tape the two ends of one link to each other, then add another ring, and another, always making sure that the writing appears on the outside of the rings so that you can read it easily. This set of "deliberate practice links" is your list of challenging tasks to perform each time you work in that subject.

> When you have mastered a task, cut out its link and add it to a set of "mastered tasks." That set of brain-links will get longer and longer as you master new challenges, and you can add new tasks to the "deliberate practice links" to have a handy list of challenging tasks you'd like to focus on.

Zella made a set of links for her guitar practice. She used one link as a title—"GUITAR"—and then made links for the deliberate practice she'd like to focus on. Two of them are new chords she needs to get nailed down: (C9 and G) and two are for other tasks she finds challenging and important at this stage: writing out the tablature of chords she knows, and working on the development of a song using the chords she knows.

Key Terms Related to Psychology

Active learning: *Active learning* means actively practicing or doing something yourself to bring what you are learning to life. Watching other people, looking at a solution, or reading a page can help you get started. But it won't do much to build your own neural structures of learning. Only actively working with the materials will help you build strong brain-links.

Active recall: *Active recall* means bringing an idea back to mind, preferably without any notes or book in front of you. Simply recalling key ideas you are learning has been shown to be a great way to understand them.

Amnesia: *Amnesia* is the inability to remember new facts or events in your life.

Cognitive load: *Cognitive load* means how much mental effort is being used in the working memory. If you have too big a cognitive load because you are being presented with too many new ideas at once, you can't take in new information very easily.

Deliberate practice: *Deliberate practice* means focusing on the material that's most difficult for you. The opposite is "lazy learning"—repeatedly practicing what's easiest.

Fact memory: We use the term *fact* to indicate a category of memory that is more abstract. Facts can be harder to store in long-term memory than *pictures*. (Psychologists call these types of long-term memories that are common knowledge, such as the names of colors and other basic facts acquired over a lifetime, "semantic" memory.)

Interleaving: *Interleaving* means practicing different aspects of what you are trying to learn so you understand the differences between the techniques. Chapter 4 in your algebra textbook may introduce you to one set of problem-solving techniques, while chapter 5 introduces you to a different set of problem-solving techniques. Interleaving means alternating between chapter 4–and chapter 5–type problems so you can see when to use the two different techniques.

Long-term memory: *Long-term memory* is like your brain's "locker"—a long-term storage space for memories. You can store lots of information in your long-term memory. *Sets of brain-links* are stored in long-term memory.

Picture memory: We use the term *picture memory* to mean a category of memories that involves pictures. Pictures are easier to store in your *long-term memory* than *facts*. (Psychologists call picture memory "episodic" memory.)

Working memory: *Working memory* is your brain's temporary storage space. You can think of working memory as being like an octopus with only four arms. This is because you can hold about four items at once in your working memory. "Arms" of your working memory can reach down into your *long-term memory* to connect with *sets of brain-links* you have created there.

SUMMING IT UP

> Looking at a solution or watching someone else practice can get you started in learning something new. But just looking or watching doesn't build your brain-links. **Actively working through a problem, or doing an activity, is what creates brain-links.**

> **You create and strengthen sets of brain-links through *deliberate practice*.** That's focused, repeated work on the more difficult parts of a concept. Don't waste much time on the easy stuff that you already know.

> ***Interleaving* is the other important part of making an expert set of brain-links.** Switch around within a subject. This will give you a sense of the topic as a whole.

Your neurons will eventually link up and you'll have completed a whole "puzzle."

> **Practice *active recall*.** Test yourself. Have someone else test you.

> ***Teach* your mom or dad or friend about an idea you find difficult.** Try to do this without notes. This is one of the best ways to strengthen your brain-links and will also make you realize where you have gaps in your knowledge.

> Remember what you learned in the first chapter—**go on picture walks.** This gets your mind ready for what it's about to work on.

CHECK YOUR UNDERSTANDING

1. Without looking back in the chapter, can you explain how a puzzle is a good metaphor for the way we piece together concepts?

2. How would you explain the idea of "interleaving" to a seven-year-old? Can you think of an example you could use to make it easy to understand?

3. What is "lazy learning"?

4. What would Superman say about reading comics when you should be practicing piano?

5. What is the special advice to help with studying math, science, and other abstract subjects?

(When you're done, you can compare your answers with the ones at the back of the book.)

Picture walk done, a few end-of-chapter questions tackled, and notebook ready for the next chapter? ☐

CHAPTER 13

ASKING YOURSELF IMPORTANT QUESTIONS

Should You Listen to Music

While You're Studying?

I want you to close your eyes. Oops! Not yet! *After* you've finished reading this paragraph. Imagine you are looking down on yourself from the ceiling. Now.

Could you see your hair? The clothes you're wearing? Did your face look like it's concentrating? What kind of learner can you see from up there?

What does "ceiling you" think of your learning today? Are you an effective learner yet? Remember your built-in lie detectors—your dendritic spines!

Becoming an Artist and a Scientist

We'd like you to become a learning scientist. What should you be studying? *You.* We want you to step away and look at what you're doing "from the ceiling."

Look at yourself from the ceiling. How is your learning going?

Your first experiment? Music. Some people say you shouldn't listen to music when you're studying. But we're all different, and we have different tastes. Do *you* find that music helps your studies? Or does it distract?

You're going to be a learning scientist, so you need to do some observations. You need to *watch* yourself learning, and think about what works and what doesn't. Some people even like to record their observations in a notebook. We know that you're a busy student, and this won't work for everyone, but here's a suggestion that you could try for a few days if you're feeling adventurous: Toward the end of each day, jot down the date. Then draw a little picture that symbolizes your day. Good or bad, just do it—no work of art needed. It should only take thirty seconds or so to draw.

What did you draw? A thumbs-up? A flower? A frog? A boot? It only matters that the picture has a meaning for *you*.

Then, if you're keeping a notebook, you could add a few notes about your learning that day. Remember, you're observing "from the ceiling." You want a calm, outsider perspective. You're being scientific about this. How did your learning go? Did you do a Pomodoro? How many? Two? Three? Was there something you did especially well? Anything you might have done better? What made a difference in your learning that day? (Incidentally, research has shown that one thing you can do to help you fall asleep faster is to make a task list for what you plan to do the next day. This takes the items out of your working memory and helps you relax and sleep better.)

If you're not a fan of the notebook idea, perhaps because that seems like extra homework, that's okay, but you could try talking to a learning buddy, or your mom or dad, about how your learning went that day. Ask yourself the same questions.

Did you listen to music, for example? If so, did you get lost in it, distracted from your studies? Or did it provide a soothing background for you? It's important for you to be honest.

As you're reflecting on your observations, try to spot patterns. Do you have better days after a good night's sleep, for example? Or after you've gone for a run? If you leave your phone on while studying, is it a distraction? Or does your phone have a Pomodoro timer you use that instead helps boost your concentration? Are you more productive when you listen to certain types of music? Or do you study better when you don't listen to music at all?

Are you wondering what scientists say about music's effects on your studies? We're just set to tell you about it. But first, here are some other unexpected factors that affect your learning.

Studying in Different Places

Think about *where* you study. Is it always in your bedroom? At the library? At a friend's house? Outside in nature? Or do you change it up? It may seem strange at first, but *it's good to change the place where you study.*[1]

Why? It has to do with your friendly attentional octopus. Real live octopuses have suckers that can help it attach to things; in our metaphor, the suckers can make your learning either "stick" or "slip."

When your attentional octopus is helping you understand material, it also picks up other random stuff. If you study geometry in the library, for example, your octopus is working with you to understand the topic. But it also picks up a little of the *feel*, *smell*, and *look* of the library at the same time.

A little library flavoring rubs onto the links.

If you always study geometry in the library, your octopus gets used to it. When you go to pull a set of geometry links out of your long-term memory, you don't realize it, but this set of brain-links has bits of "library" stuck to it. Your octopus expects the geometry links to be library flavored.

So what?

Here's the thing. You don't normally take tests in the library.

If you've always studied in the library, but your tests are in classrooms, your octopus can get confused. In the classroom, your octopus can have trouble finding the geometry links, because there are no library flavors around to guide it. You may end up doing worse on the exam.

So, if you can, it's better to study in a *variety* of places! We know that schools don't always give you a lot of choice about where to study, but if possible, mix it up at home by studying in different rooms.

That way, your attentional octopus ends up getting used to finding things in your long-term memory locker *regardless* of where you're studying. If you study geometry in the library on Monday, at home on Tuesday, and at the park on Wednesday—or even just in different rooms on different days—your octopus gets used to finding your geometry links wherever you are. You can do better on your test!

Get creative and develop your own tricks to shake things up. Move your chair sometimes to a different part of the room. Take notes with a different color pen. Move your lamp. Anything to switch your learning up a bit!

The Problem with Auditory Versus Visual Learning Styles

Researchers agree that people process information in different ways. This has led to talk about "auditory," or "visual," or "kinesthetic"* learners. The idea is that some people learn best by listening, others by picturing things, others by touching.

Unfortunately, what research has shown is that relying on a "preferred learning style"—that is, using one sense instead of several—*can weaken your ability to learn in other ways.*[2] For example, if you think you're an "auditory learner," you try to learn by listening. The result? You get less practice with reading. How are you going to do well on tests, for example, if you don't practice reading?

We learn best when we use several *different* senses—hearing, seeing, and, perhaps especially, being able to feel with our hands. At deep levels in your brain, you see *and* hear. You see *and* smell. You hear *and* touch. When your brain creates its impressions of the world, you want as many senses involved as possible.

So whenever you're learning anything, try to take advantage of *all* your senses. Don't think of yourself as having a preferred learning style. Think of yourself as an "all-inclusive" learner. If you imagine *hearing* a famous person from history *speaking* to you, or you *visualize* a chemical, that counts as *multisensory learning*, which is the most effective kind. For everyone.

---

* It's pronounced "kin-es-THET-ick." Kinesthetic means learning through touching or feeling. For example, you can learn about different materials like honey, a sponge, or a steel screw, not only by looking at them, but by feeling them.

Sleep—It's Even *More* Important Than You Think!

Here's one for your learning journal. Did you get enough sleep? This will shock you, but just being *awake* creates nasty toxic products in your brain. The longer you're awake, the more the toxins build up. What an awful thought!

It's not as bad as it sounds. Once you go to sleep, your brain cells shrink, and the poisonous toxins are washed away through the gaps.[3] When you wake up, the poisons have gone. Just like a computer can be rebooted to clear away errors, your brain is rebooted when you wake up from a good night's sleep. This is your overnight upgrade!

If you don't sleep enough, there isn't time for all the toxins to be cleaned away. You start the day groggy, blocked, and unable to think clearly. Your neurons can't grow new synapses, either. There's been no time for your mental mouse to run along the pathways and make new connections. Fail!

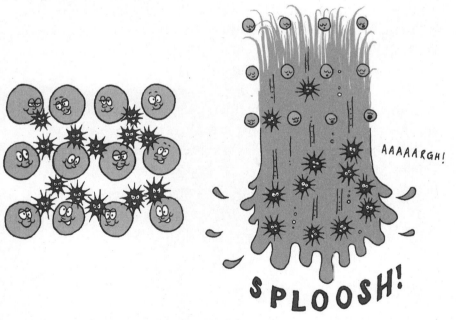

AAAAARGH!

SPLOOSH!

When you go to sleep, your neurons shrink, which allows the toxins to be washed away.

Sleep is the ultimate diffuse mode. Ideas, images, and pieces of knowledge flow around your brain freely. Different areas of the brain link up, connect creatively, and work on problems together. People sometimes talk about "sleeping on it" when they're not sure about something. Your sleeping brain is good at figuring out what to do even when you're not focused on it.

And incidentally, a nap can also help your learning. Much like ordinary nighttime sleep, a nap allows the information that's temporarily been stored in the hippocampus to be moved into long-term memory locations in other places in your brain. This movement "empties" your hippocampus so it can more easily hold the new information you want to pour into it after your nap. But don't make the mistake of thinking that a series of naps during the day makes up for a good long sleep each evening. It doesn't.

This may spark the question of how much sleep you should be getting. Although people differ, in general you should have at least eight hours a night reserved for "sleep opportunity time"—that is, time to both fall asleep and be asleep.*[4] These eight hours of sleep opportunity time should be consistent during the week—it's not the kind of thing you try to catch up on over the weekends. **Sleep is the best thing you can do to retune yourself each day and keep yourself healthy.** Teens and younger people often need even more than eight hours per night.

To help yourself get a good sleep, after dusk rolls around, avoid anything that emits blue light, like iPads, computer screens, and smartphones. You can also download blue-light-blocking apps.

Not sleeping enough can have long-term consequences that are similar to eating arsenic. Lack of sleep allows toxic products to build up all over your body, makes you more prone to getting sick,

---

* As sleep researcher Matthew Walker explains, due to our genes, about 40 percent of us are "morning types" who like to wake up early. Another 30 percent are "night owls" who like to go to bed late and wake up late. The rest are a mix of both types. Unlike adults, teenagers often have internal "sleep clocks" that move them toward night owl status. This can make it difficult for teenagers to go to sleep early, even when they want to. Unfortunately, many schools have too-early start times that do not allow teenagers to get the sleep that they both want and need. A few schools have shifted to later start times, and they've seen significant increases in test scores as a result.

to getting cancer, and to all sorts of mental problems. Lack of sleep also stops the growth of new neurons and synapses, making it far harder for you to learn.

So note in your learning journal, if you are keeping one, how much sleep you had the night before and keep track of how you feel. This will help you get a better sense of how well you are doing in the sleep department. If you are tired and find yourself falling asleep during the day, you definitely are not getting enough sleep.

And another thing. If you do a little bit of focused work just before going to sleep, you're more likely to dream about it. And dreaming about your studies can help you on your tests. It sticks better.[5]

Make sleep a high priority. Don't work late the night before a test. It's harder to do well. One Pomodoro with a fresh brain is worth three with a tired one!

Eat Your Frogs First!

"Eat your frogs first" means it's best to get started on the unpleasant or difficult things first in your study session. That way, you can take a break and work on something else if you get stuck. This lets your diffuse mode work in the background to "unstick" you when you return. You might even finish your difficult task at the beginning of your work period, which feels great. (Of course, if you like eating frogs, you will need to change the metaphor. Some people like to think of this as "Save your cookies for last!")

Set a Quitting Time

One last tip. It helps a lot if you are able to set a quitting time for your studies each day. We know that school controls a lot of this, but when you're working on your homework, plan to stop by a certain time if you can.

Cal Newport, for example, had a firm 5:00 P.M. quitting time throughout his college studies. He ended up getting his doctorate (that's the most advanced kind of university degree) in computer science from MIT. This is one of the world's best universities, so it worked well for him. (You might want to check out some of his books, such as *How to Become a Straight-A Student*.) Cal insists that he was not a natural superstar. Instead, he found that setting a firm quitting time allowed him to focus intently on his studies during the day. He was then able to relax and enjoy life with his friends in the evening. Cal reduced his stress levels by learning to keep intent focus when he was studying.

Cal recommends a shutdown ritual he uses when he's removing himself from work. You might do something similar. Pretend you're an airplane pilot. At the appointed time, say a countdown that ends with "Systems off!"

One exception. Before you go to sleep, you *can* make a few notes in your learning journal or think back over your day. It's also okay to take a last peek at something you're trying to reinforce. This fuels your dreaming and your learning. But try to stay away from backlit screens, like those on a computer or smartphone, for at least an hour or two before bedtime. Backlit screens send light signals to your brain that say "Wake up!" This can make it hard for you to fall asleep.

Chapter Wrap-Up: Back to Music

We've covered a lot in this chapter. Now that we're ending, we promised to let you know what research has to say about listening to music.

Here's the conclusion: Scientists aren't sure![6] Sometimes, and for some people, music *can* be helpful. But sometimes music can fool you into thinking it's helpful when it's actually harmful.

This is why it's so important to become a learning scientist.

Observing your learning as if you are a scientist will allow you to see what effect music and other influences have on you.

The only guidance that research provides about music is this. It seems that your attentional octopus can be more easily distracted by loud music, and by music with words in it. The words fill one of your octopus's arms, making it less efficient. But quieter music with no words can sometimes be helpful, depending on what you are studying. One thing to keep in mind is that there probably won't be music when you're taking a test—unless you happen to be close to the music room at school!

The bottom line is that if you want to listen to music when you are studying, it may be okay. But be careful. You will need to try this out for yourself and see what works for you. Be honest with yourself.

Now You Try! Think Like a Learning Scientist

Today's a great day to start a new habit: reflecting on your learning. Scientists observe things carefully and try to spot patterns. You need to do the same. Whether you use a journal or just get into the habit of thinking back over the day, the important thing is to think about it. Remember to observe as if you were watching "from the ceiling." After a while, you'll become so used to it, you'll be able to see your day's activities in your mind's eye even when your eyes are open!

If you've had a quiz or test that day, it can be especially valuable to think like a learning scientist. If you did well, what did you do right? If you didn't do very well, what went wrong? What parts didn't you know well? How did you study those parts? What can you do to do better next time?

Here's a sample of what your journal might hold, or the sorts of things you might think about at the tail end of the day:

My Learning Journal—a Sample Page*[7]

Date: _____ Your Symbol for the Day:

How did I set myself up?

How long did I sleep the previous night? _____ hours

How long did I exercise today? _____ minutes

What food did I eat today? ❏ Fruits ❏ Vegetables ❏ Nuts
❏ Protein-Rich Foods ❏ No Junk

Where? What? When?

My School Bag and My Locker

New Stuff I Learned:	Old Stuff I Recalled and Reviewed:

Where did I study?

Place 1: _____   Place 2: _____

Place 3: _____

Pomodoros I did today (tick off): 🍅 🍅 🍅 🍅 🍅 🍅

Some Smart Things I Did Today:

Swallowed any frogs?

Tackled any tests?

Taught someone else?

To-do list made for the day?

My system shutdown time: _____

LEARNING HOW TO LEARN

_____

* You can find a copy of this learning journal page at https://barbaraoakley.com/books/learning-how-to-learn.

Pause and Recall

What were the main ideas of this chapter? You can recall them where you are currently sitting, but then try recalling the ideas again in a different room, or better yet, when you are outside.

Check this box when you're done: ❏

SUMMING IT UP

› Everybody's different. That's why it's important to **become your own personal learning scientist.** You can see what works best in *your* learning. Think like a scientist and start looking for patterns in what works and what doesn't work for you.

› Music can be either helpful or harmful when it comes to learning. Look "from the ceiling" at how music affects your studies.

› **Study in different places when you can.** This allows your attentional octopus to be comfortable when it takes a test in a room that's not the one you studied in.

› **Try to learn using a variety of senses.** Your eyes, your ears, your hands—even your nose can help you learn. You learn best when you use *all* your senses.

› Sleep not only helps build new synaptic connections—it also washes away toxins!

› **Eat your frogs first.** Start with the harder materials first so you can take a break and use diffuse mode if you need to.

› When you can, set a firm daily **quitting time** to allow you to concentrate more intently when you are working.

CHECK YOUR UNDERSTANDING

1. This chapter described certain types of music that are not so helpful when you are trying to study. Retell these findings in your own words.

2. Explain why it is a good idea to study in a variety of places.

3. What's wrong with believing you have a particular learning style?

4. How could you use sight, hearing, and "feeling" at the same time you are learning something abstract, like math?

5. What does sleep have to do with toxins in the brain?

6. Explain the saying "Eat your frogs first."

7. What is the best way (as mentioned in this chapter) to help you concentrate more effectively when you are working?

(When you're done, you can compare your answers with the ones at the back of the book.)

Picture walk done, a few end-of-chapter questions tackled, and notebook ready for the next chapter? ☐

CHAPTER 14

LEARNING SURPRISES

Pssst . . .

Your Worst Traits Can Be Your Best Traits!

Have you ever seen someone's hand rocket up with the answer in class? When meanwhile, you're struggling to understand what the teacher just asked? Race Car Brain already has the *answer*, while you didn't even understand the *question*.

It's easy to think that if you're a slower learner, then learning's not for you. But we've got some surprises in store. If you're slower than others, you can do just as well. Sometimes even *better* than fast learners.

How can that be?

We'll get to that. In this chapter, we're going to talk about a lot of learning surprises. Sometimes what you believed about learning just isn't true. Let's look at video games.

Video Games

Do your parents give you a hard time about video games? Lots of parents do. There *are* some bad things about video games, as you'll soon see. But here's a surprise for your parents. Some types of video games can actually be helpful for your learning. In fact, certain video games can be helpful for your parents, too![1]

Action video games are great for *focusing*. While you're having fun, you're also learning to concentrate. When you play an action video game, your mental mouse runs up and down a centrally important brain path. It's the "focus" path in your brain, and it gets wider as you use it more. Becoming a strong video gamer means that when you turn your attention to something, you can *really* focus.*

---

* I should point out that video games do not make your working memory bigger. Making a bigger working memory is like adding more arms to an octopus, which is hard to do. If you see advertisements for games that give you a bigger working memory, you should be suspicious. Right now, researchers don't know how to help people build bigger working memories. If you don't have a good working memory, read on. You'll learn that you have some special benefits!

Incidentally, it's a reasonable guess that Nobel Prize winner Santiago Ramón y Cajal's underlying memory challenge was that he had a poor working memory. As Santiago described in his autobiography, his father was very good at using memory tricks to store information in long-term memory. Santiago probably learned some of those tricks from his father. But Santiago's father *wasn't* able to help his son improve his working memory, because we still don't know how to improve working memory even today.

This may sound bad for Santiago, but it really wasn't. Santiago's poor working memory was, it seems, part of the magic that allowed Santiago to see the simple underlying principles of neuroanatomy that "geniuses" had missed. So, again, if you have a poor working memory, you may have to work harder on occasion to keep up. But it can also sometimes be a wonderful gift that can allow you to see more simply and clearly than other "smarter" people!

Action video games also improve your vision in some ways. You learn to pick out details better than people who don't play action-style video games. You can even see better in the fog!

It's not only action video games that are helpful. Games like Tetris can build your spatial ("SPAY-shell") abilities. That means you can learn to rotate things more easily in your mind's eye. This is an important skill in math and science.

Not every type of video game is helpful. The Sims, for example, is a "life simulation video game." Sounds good, but this kind of game doesn't allow you to practice what psychologists call "attentional control." If you want to improve your focused or spatial thinking, research says you should stick to action or spatial kinds of video games.

The downside to video gaming is that it can be addictive. As with exercise, eating, and even learning itself, common sense is key. If video gaming is interfering with other parts of your life, it's time to cut back. Even if gaming is your absolute passion, you now know that exercise and taking breaks can help you perform better. So can opening your mind to other, very different, types of learning.

We mentioned that video games could also be useful for adults. If you're into action-style games, introduce them to your parents! Yes, action-style video games can help improve your parents' ability to focus and concentrate, even while they're growing older. There are even action video games that are on track to be approved as "drugs" by the Federal Drug Administration. They can improve older people's thinking abilities.

Al enjoys a video game with his son, Jacob.

So the next time your mom or dad tells you that video gaming is bad for you, show this book to them. Too much video gaming is definitely bad! But *some* can be good. And if your parents decide to join you, it could be healthy for them, too!

Learn Something *Completely* Different

We said that if you are a passionate video gamer, it can help your gaming to learn or do something *completely* different from video games. Oil painting, pole vaulting, learning to speak Finnish, juggling, Japanese manga—as long as it's *different*, it can aid in unexpected ways with your video gaming.

In fact, if you're passionate about *anything*, you can become even better at your passion if you also learn a little bit about something quite different.

Why?

You can get stuck in what we call "rut think."* Your mind gets so used to running along certain neural pathways that it can't easily change. You become less flexible in your thinking.

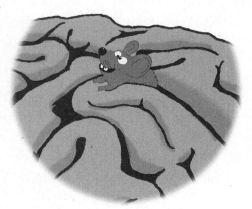

"Rut think"

---

* Psychologists call this general idea "Einstellung" or "functional fixedness." But these can be hard words to remember, so we prefer "rut think."

Here's another way to look at it. If you decide to get *great* at something, you tend to want to spend all your time doing it. But the fact is, everybody else who is trying to get great at it is doing *the same thing*. So how can you do better than they are if you're doing exactly what they're doing?

Ready to be surprised again? The way to get better is to strike out in a completely different direction. You learn about something else. Anything else. *Whatever* you learn, your brain finds a way to make those ideas useful for your main passion, often through metaphor.

This important learning idea is called *transfer*. The brain-links you create in one area allow you to more easily build links in a different area. Learning to hit a baseball, for example, can help you with many ball games—and ultimately can help you better understand physics. Learning physics can assist you in learning economics, and how to create more beautiful pottery. *Transferring* ideas from one subject or activity to another helps you to be more creative. It's like a template you can adapt from one area to another.

How to Take Notes

Here's another learning surprise. People often think that the best way to take notes is to type them out. After all, it can be faster to type than to write by hand. And the notes are neater.

Nope. Writing notes by hand is better. Even if you have lousy handwriting.*

Remember, you need to make a *set of brain-links* out of the key ideas. Amazingly, if you just type what you are hearing, the words flow onto the page without creating a set of links. Into the ears, out of the hands, with no deep brain work in between.

If you write by hand, you have to do some thinking about what

---

* If you happen to have a condition that makes it tough for you to write by hand, you can still do okay if you type your notes. But avoid falling into the mindless trap of just typing what you hear. You need to slow your typing so you can summarize the key ideas instead of just typing everything that flows into your ears.

goes onto the paper. This helps start a set of brain-links. Your dendritic spines begin to grow. If you review your notes one last time before you go to sleep, you can make your dendritic spines grow even better while you sleep!

A good approach to note taking is to draw a line down one side of the page, about one-third of the way from the edge. Write your first notes in the larger section. Then later, when you review them, write even briefer key points in the smaller section. Then look away and see if you can recall those key points. Test yourself. Practice pulling on those links!

There's no magical formula for note taking. The basic idea is to pick out key points so that you can review them and strengthen your brain-links.

Do You Have a Poor Working Memory? Congratulations!

Here's another learning surprise. *Poor* working memories are sometimes better than *strong* working memories.

How so?

Some people have fantastic working memories. Their attentional octopus may have eight or even more arms, and their octopus's tentacles are incredibly sticky. They can hold a *lot* in mind, and it *stays* in mind. What's not to like about that?

But a poor working memory can also have upsides. If you have only three arms on your attentional octopus, for example, you have to work harder to make brain-links out of the key ideas. You don't have enough arms on your octopus to hold many thoughts in mind, so you have to figure out ways to simplify and link the ideas together.

This means the sets of brain-links created by a person with poor working memory can contain surprisingly elegant simplifications and creative leaps.[2] The person with a strong working memory can find this kind of elegant, creative simplification harder to do. Their strong working memory means they don't need to find ways to simplify.

People with poor working memories often find thoughts slipping from their mind. Sounds bad, right? But it can be good! Research shows that when one thought slips from the mind, another pops in. People with poor working memory can be especially creative! This creativity is particularly noticeable in people who have attentional "disorders" (we think the term should be "advantages") like ADHD.[3]

People with poor working memory and focus sometimes have to work harder than others to make brain-links. But the trade-off is that it can be easier for them to be more creative. They see elegant shortcuts and have ideas that others miss. The trade-off can be worth it!

Hiker Brains Versus Race Car Brains

So we're gradually seeing how a person who thinks slowly can sometimes do better than a "race car brain" person.

Think about it this way. A person with a race car for a brain can get to the finish line faster. In other words, they can figure out the answers to questions more quickly. The slower thinker, on the other hand, can get to the answer, but much more slowly. (Keep in mind that some people can be race cars in some subjects and hikers in others.)

For the race car brain person, everything goes by in a blur. They're thinking fast, and not necessarily worrying about the details. The "hiker brain" person, on the other hand, moves much more slowly. While they move slowly, they can reach out and touch the leaves on the trees, smell the pine in the air, hear the birds singing, and see the little rabbit trails.

This means that in some ways, the hiker brain can see more deeply than the race car brain.

So if you have a hiker brain on some or many subjects, be happy. It may take you more time to learn something than the race car brain. But you can still learn it just fine—in fact, you can learn more richly and deeply. If you have a race car brain, you can also be happy. But you'll also need to be careful not to steer off track, because it can be hard for you to get back on. We'll talk more about this later.

In the next chapter, we'll move on to one of the most important chapters of the book. How to prepare for tests!

> **Action video games can improve your ability to focus.** They can also improve your vision. They can be especially useful for older people, to help keep their focus strong.

> **Spatial video games can improve your ability to rotate objects mentally**—an important skill in math and science.

> One drawback of video games is that, like any other pleasurable activity, they can become **addictive.** Use common sense to avoid overdoing it.

> **To build your mental flexibility, learn about something completely different from your passion.** You'll see links that lead to creative new ideas, which help with your passion. Learning something very different also helps you to avoid "rut think."

> **Take notes by hand.** It enables you to make brain-links out of the key ideas more easily.

> **A poor working memory can be a good thing.** It can allow you to:

  ◗ See elegant simplifications that others miss.

  ◗ Be more creative.

> **"Slow" thinkers can understand a subject or problem just as well as "fast" thinkers.** Slow thinkers may need more time, but they can sometimes actually understand the subject *better* than fast thinkers.

Now You Try! Write It Down

Physiotherapists ("FIZZ-ee-o-THER-a-pists") help treat people's physical problems by using movement. Spanish physiotherapist Elena Benito says, "As a physiotherapist, I know that the hand has many connections in our brain. Each handwritten letter sends extraordinary amounts of information back and forth between our brain and our hand."

Elena Benito knows how important movement can be in helping us to understand something difficult we are trying to learn.

Elena advises:

"When you don't understand some item you are studying, maybe a mathematical formula, or a really long sentence . . . just write it down, once, twice . . . Sometimes this helps you make sense of it. Writing it down can help you jump mental barriers and install the information deeply in another place in our brains where it is processed differently."

Next time you encounter something you find difficult to understand, try Elena's trick. Write it down!

Pause and Recall

What were the main ideas of this chapter? Which idea is most important—or are there several competing equally important ideas? Close the book and look away as you try this.

Check this box when you're done: ❑

CHECK YOUR UNDERSTANDING

1. Which two types of video games seem to improve your thinking? Why?

2. What is a bad aspect of video gaming that was high-lighted in this chapter?

3. What is the key idea behind good note taking?

4. What is "rut think"?

5. If you want to be more creative and get better at some-thing you are passionate about, what should you do?

6. What is *transfer*?

7. Explain why a poor working memory can help you see elegant simplifications that others miss, and also be more creative.

8. Give an example of a subject or skill where a "slow" learner can learn something just as well as a "fast" learner, even if it might take a little longer.

(When you're done, you can compare your answers with the ones at the back of the book.)

Picture walk done, a few end-of-chapter questions tackled, and notebook ready for the next chapter? ☐

CHAPTER 15

HOW TO DO WELL
ON TESTS

One important caution. **If you've skipped the rest of the book and just jumped directly to this chapter, you're not going to benefit nearly as much as if you read the full book.**

You are reading this chapter because tests matter. That's a fact of life. In an ideal world we would all learn things just because they're interesting and we really want to know about them. There's so much more to education than just passing official tests. But tests are an important part of showing yourself (and other people) that you have learned something well. They can be important stepping-stones in life as you move from school to college, or from college into a profession.

Tests can even be fun. Honestly!

Research shows that tests are one of the best ways to help you learn. You can learn more in one hour of taking a test than in one hour of studying.[1] (During a test, we try hard to recall whatever little bit we can about the topic. When we're just studying, not so much.)

Remember how we talked about the importance of recall? Pulling on those brain-links when you're dragging something up from long-term memory? We know that recall strengthens your learning. It turns out that recall is just a little test that you're giving yourself.

When I was a young professor, I learned a lot from a great engineering educator named Richard Felder. Dr. Felder taught me a lot about how to teach well. He wants to help students to be successful.

Here is a test preparation checklist like one Dr. Felder developed to enable students to be successful on tests.[2] How do you use this checklist? Simply do whatever it takes to be able to answer "Yes" to most of the questions.

Test Preparation Checklist*

Answer "Yes" only if you *usually* do these things:

1. Did you get a reasonable night's **sleep** before the test? (If your answer is "No," then your answers to the rest of the questions may not matter.)	____Yes ____No
2. Did you **review** your notes from class not long after you took them? Did you use *active recall* during your review to see if you could easily pull to mind the key ideas?	____Yes ____No
3. **Did you study a little bit on most days** instead of waiting until the last minute and cramming right before the test?	____Yes ____No
4. Did you focus carefully during your study sessions, doing your best to **avoid distractions** except when you were taking a break?	____Yes ____No
5. Did you study in **different locations**?	____Yes ____No
6. **Did you read your textbook or class worksheets carefully?** (Just fishing around for the answer to what you're working on doesn't count.) While you were reading, did you avoid too much underlining and highlighting your textbook? Did you make brief notes about the book's key ideas and then look away to see if you could recall them?	____Yes ____No

_____

* A copy of this checklist can be downloaded from https://barbaraoakley.com/books/learning-how-to-learn.

7. If your studies involved working problems, **did you *actively* work and rework key examples by yourself**, so you turned them into *sets of brain-links* and could rapidly call the solution to mind? _____Yes _____No

8. **Did you discuss homework problems with classmates**, or at least check your solutions with others? _____Yes _____No

9. **Did you actively work every homework problem yourself?** _____Yes _____No

10. **Did you talk to your teachers, or to other students who could help,** when you were having trouble with your understanding? _____Yes _____No

11. Did you spend most of your study time focusing on the material you found harder? That is, did you do **deliberate practice**? _____Yes _____No

12. Did you **interleave** your studies? In other words, did you practice *when* to use different techniques? _____Yes _____No

13. Did you explain key ideas to yourself, and perhaps to others, using **funny metaphors and images**? _____Yes _____No

14. Did you take occasional breaks from your studies that included some **physical activity**? _____Yes _____No

TOTAL: _____Yes _____No

The more "Yes" responses you recorded, the better your preparation for the test. If you recorded three or more "No" responses, think seriously about making some changes in how you prepare for the next test.

The Hard-Start Technique: Learning When to Disconnect

For years, students have been told to start a test with the easiest problems first.

Neuroscience says this is *not* a good idea. (Unless you haven't studied at all. Then you should take whatever easy points you can get!)

When you begin your test, here's what you should do. Start by quickly looking it over. Make a little checkmark beside what you think are the hardest problems. Then pick one of the hard problems and start working on it. Yes, that's right—a *hard* problem. (Eat your frogs first!)

Just work on this problem a minute or two—however long it takes until you feel like you're stuck.

As soon as you feel yourself getting stuck, leave it. Look for an easier problem to boost your confidence. Do that next. And then maybe another one.

Then go back to the hard problem. You may now be able to make some progress.

How come?

Doing the "hard-start" technique allows you to use your brain as a sort of double processor. Your diffuse mode can take over on the hard problem as soon as you drop your focus on it. While the focused mode is tackling the easier problem, the diffuse mode works in the background on the other, harder problem. If you wait until the end of your test session to focus on the hardest problems, your focus prevents the diffuse mode from going to work.

You can use this hard-start technique in your homework, also. A common mistake on homework is to start a hard problem and then keep working on it too long without making progress. Some work, even a little frustration, is okay. But if the frustration goes on too long, you need to *disconnect!* How long is too long to work on a problem? Maybe five or ten minutes—it depends on the subject and your age.

The hard-start technique is a good one for both tests and home-work because it allows you to use your brain's two modes more effectively. It also gives you valuable practice in *disconnecting* and moving on to problems you *can* solve. Disconnecting can be one of a student's biggest challenges on a test—you can run out of time even though there were other, easier problems that you could have solved.

On a test, you may want to disconnect more quickly when you find yourself stuck than when you're doing homework. A general rule is, if you're stuck for more than a minute or two on a test, move on!

The Best Stress? Test Stress!

Research has shown that the more you practice active recall in the weeks before a test, the less that stress will bother you when you take the test.[3] So if tests stress you out, it's especially important for you to practice recall in your studies.

Let's face it, though: It's easy to get stressed when you sit down to take a test. Your palms get sweaty, your heart races, and you get an anxious feeling in the stomach. This happens because your body releases chemicals when you are under stress. Surprisingly, these stressful feelings can help you do *better* on the test.[4] When you might notice anxious feelings, try to shift your perspective. Instead of thinking, "This test makes me nervous," try to think, "This test has got me excited to do my best!"[5]

When you get nervous, you tend to breathe from the top of your chest.*[6] This "shallow" breathing doesn't give you enough oxygen.

---

* Shallow breathing seems like a bad idea. So why do people do it when they get nervous? It relates to the fact that eyes are natural motion detectors. By *freezing*, an

You begin to feel panic that has nothing to do with the test. You just aren't getting enough oxygen! If you tend to get nervous before a test, it can help for you to practice deep breathing.

To do deep breathing, put one hand on your belly. It should move out when you breathe in, just like the picture shows. Try to imagine your breath also expanding your back, as if you had sails. Practice deep breathing in the days before a test, so you get used to it. Just stand sideways in front of a mirror to try it out for thirty seconds or so.

Shallow breathing is at the top of your chest. Deep breathing is in the lower part of your chest. Deep breathing helps reduce feelings of panic.

A Few Final Suggestions for Test Success

Watch out for "rut think." Once you've written a solution to a problem, it's easy to think it must be right.

When you've already gone through the test once (if you have time), try to trick your mind into looking at the test again with fresh eyes. Blink and look away to try to take yourself briefly into diffuse mode. Check the problems in a different order from the way you did them. If possible, ask yourself, "Does this answer make sense?" If

---

animal can sometimes avoid detection even when it is in plain sight. Breathing shallowly, or even momentarily holding the breath, can help an animal or a person be as motionless as possible.

The next time you point out a bird or animal to a friend, watch your friend's reaction. Even when you are pointing straight at what you want your friend to see, your friend often can't see it until it moves.

you've just calculated that you need ten billion gallons of water to fill your classroom's aquarium, something's wrong!

Sometimes you can study hard, but the examination just doesn't go your way. If you have prepared carefully, however, Lady Luck tends to smile.

Pause, Recall, and Reflect

What were the main ideas of this chapter? How will you prepare differently for tests after having read this chapter?
Check this box when you're done: ❑

SUMMING IT UP

> Use a **test preparation checklist** to make sure you are preparing properly for tests.

> Use the **_hard-start technique_**. If you've studied well for a test, start the test with a _hard_ problem. Then pull yourself away when you find you are getting stuck and work on another, easier problem. You can go back to work on the harder problem again later in the test. You can often make more progress than if you tackled the hard problem at the end of the test, when you have little time.

> Your body releases chemicals when you're excited or nervous. **How you interpret your feelings makes a difference**. If you shift your thinking from "This test has made me afraid" to "This test has got me excited to do my best!" it can improve your performance.

> **Breathe deeply from the belly** for a few breaths if you feel panicky before or during a test.

> **It's easy to make mistakes on a test.** Your mind can trick you into thinking that what you've done is correct, even if it isn't. This means that, whenever possible, you should

blink, shift your attention, and then double-check your answers using a big-picture perspective, asking yourself, "Does this really make sense?" Try to review the problems in a different order from when you first completed them.

> Whatever else you do, get the best **sleep** as you can before a test.

Now You Try! Create Your Own Test Questions

A good way to prepare for a test is to try to think like a teacher. Make up some questions that you think the teacher might ask. If you want, try this exercise with a friend who is also studying for the same test. You will be surprised at how often your questions match up with your friend's. And you'll be even more surprised at how often the questions you've created show up on the test!

CHECK YOUR UNDERSTANDING

1. What is the most important preparation step for taking a test? (Hint: If you don't take this step, nothing else may matter.)

2. How would you know when to leave a difficult problem on a test when you are using the hard-start technique?

3. Describe two techniques to calm yourself if you begin to feel panicked before a test.

4. What kind of mental tricks can you use to help yourself catch wrong answers on a test?

(When you're done, you can compare your answers with the ones at the back of the book.)

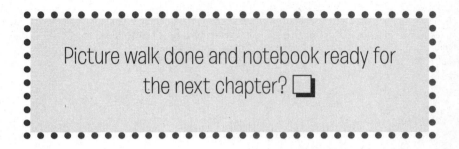

Picture walk done and notebook ready for the next chapter? ☐

CHAPTER 16

GOING FROM
"HAVE TO"
TO "GET TO"

Remember Santiago Ramón y Cajal? The "bad boy" who became a neuroscientist? We told you he was no genius. And yet, in the end, he won a Nobel Prize. As we mentioned, sometimes Santiago felt bad because he couldn't learn very fast and his memory wasn't so good. But in the end, he noticed that he had some advantages. These advantages sometimes helped him to do even better than geniuses. What could these advantages have been?*

We'll get to Santiago's advantages soon. In the meantime, congratulations! You have worked your way through learning discoveries that will help you for the rest of your life. You've also put up with a lot of zany metaphors. Electric four-armed octopuses, pinball-playing zombies, mice in your head-forest, brain-links, synaptic vacuum cleaners . . . It's been a regular cartoon network!

---

* If you *are* a genius, can you still find a way to incorporate some of Santiago's approaches?

We're a regular cartoon network!

So, great job! You've let your imagination go to work in learning some challenging science. I hope all those metaphors helped.

In this chapter, I want to revisit the main lessons of the book. After all, you know by now that repetition is one of the keys to learning.

But first I want to ask you an important question.

What's the point?

Really. I mean it. What's the point of all this learning? Why should you bother at all? From one perspective, we're just tiny little specks on a rock in the middle of an unimaginably vast universe.

Before you read on, I would like for you to try to answer that question: what's the point of learning *anything*? Try to answer this in as many different ways as you can. Aim for five reasons. Give yourself some thinking time. Find someone to explain your ideas to, and see what they say. Or you could try to write your ideas down. At the very least, think through what your answer would be in your head. Then turn the page to see some ideas that people might give.

Here are some of the things people *might* say about the "point" of learning:

> You *have* to learn because otherwise your mom or dad won't let you go out to play.
> You have to learn because otherwise your teacher will put you in detention.
> You have to learn because the law says so.
> You have to learn so you can graduate, go to college, and get a job.
> You have to learn so you can keep your options open for the future.
> You *get* to learn so you can go on and follow your passions.
> You get to learn so you can discover more about the mysteries of the universe.
> You get to learn so you can fulfill more of your amazing potential each week.
> You get to learn so you can help humanity solve some of the world's problems.
> You get to learn because you are an inquisitive human being.

Of course, there are other possible answers. But in a way *all* of the above are true.

Did you notice what I did halfway through the list? I switched from "you *have* to learn" to "you *get* to learn." I changed it from an obligation—something you have no choice about—to a privilege. That is, something you're lucky to be able to do. It's both. You *will* get detention if you don't do your homework. So, unless you like detention, that's a valid reason to do your homework. But it's not an inspiring reason to study. It works a lot better when you can see *positive* reasons for taking an interest in your learning, rather than just avoiding punishment.

Lucky to learn!

We find ourselves on this mysterious rock called Earth, in a particular place and time. And we have (probably) the most advanced technology in the universe *within our skulls*. (Unless there are aliens who have even more extraordinary intelligence than you and me—in which case it will be pretty interesting learning about them!) But wouldn't it be a crazy waste of our time on Earth not to make the most of the astonishing tool between our ears?

The younger you are when you learn how to learn more effectively, the longer you have through your life to enjoy the benefits. Learning is a privilege. In some parts of the world, children have no access at all to books or computers or teachers. I believe that we owe it to those people who don't have access to school to make the most of our opportunities. I want to encourage you in your learning for *all* of those reasons, and more. After all, as Terry says, you never know when your learning is going to come in handy.

Learn how to learn so you can follow your passions. But don't *just* follow your passions. That was my mistake when I was young. There's a lot of learning you can do that will open doors you can't yet imagine. *Broaden* your passions—learn and enjoy new subjects beyond the one you originally thought you could learn. You'll put yourself in a better place for whatever life may throw your way. The world is changing quickly, and it's going to be changing even faster. Learning how to learn is one of the very best abilities you can have.

What to Do and What *Not* to Do in Your Learning

Now, back to the main lessons of the book.

You know that *recall* is one of the best ways to learn. So here's my second challenge of the chapter. See if you can make a list of what *you* think are the main lessons from this book. You can include ideas to help your learning, as well as pitfalls to avoid.

What are your top five favorite ideas from the book? No peeking until you've got at least five in mind! Don't worry if you have to strain your brain to come up with these. Your attentional octopus hasn't grabbed these brain-links very often yet, so it's just getting used to them. Don't worry if your listing looks a little different from mine. If you have some of the same key ideas, that's what counts.*

Here's my list of some of the top ideas in the book to help your learning:

1. Make use of both the intense **focused** and relaxed **diffuse** modes. If you are getting frustrated, it's time to switch to another topic. Or get some physical exercise!

2. Create **sets of brain-links** with practice, repetition, and recall. Practice important problems so you can easily recall each step. Solutions, concepts, and techniques should flow like songs in your mind.

3. **Interleave.** Don't just keep practicing with slight changes in the same basic technique. Switch back and forth between different techniques. This will allow you to see *when* to use a technique. Books usually don't help you interleave. You will have to practice skipping back and forth between the ideas in different chapters yourself.

---

* You can find the list "10 top ideas to help your learning, and 10 pitfalls to avoid" at https://barbaraoakley.com/books/learning-how-to-learn.

4. **Space out your learning.** Practice over at least several days. This gives time for your new synapses to form.

5. **Exercise!** Exercise feeds your neurons. It also allows you to grow new and stronger synapses.

6. **Test** yourself. Have others test you. Teach others. All of these are related to *recall*. Testing and recall are the best ways to strengthen your learning.

7. Use **funny pictures and metaphors** to speed your learning. Start using memory palaces.

8. Use the **Pomodoro Technique** to build your ability to focus and relax. Just turn off all distractions, set the timer to 25 minutes, focus, and then reward yourself.

9. **Eat your frogs first.** Start your most difficult work first. That way you can either finish it or take a break to let your diffuse mode help you.

10. **Find ways to learn *actively*, outside of your usual classes.** Look online for other explanations. Read other books. Join a club. If you don't find a club in the subject that interests you, see if you can start one.

And here are ten pitfalls to avoid in your learning:

1. **Not getting enough sleep.** Sleep makes your brain-links stronger. It washes away toxins in your brain. If you don't get a good night's sleep before a test, *nothing else you have done will matter.*

2. **Passive reading and rereading.** You need to practice *active recall*, not just let your eyes pass over the same material.

3. **Highlighting or underlining.** Don't be fooled! Just highlighting or underlining big chunks of text doesn't put anything in your head. Make brief notes about the key concepts you are reading. Do this in the margin or on a piece of paper. These notes help you create *brain-links* of the key concepts.

4. **Glancing at the solution to a problem** and thinking you understand it. You need to solve the problem yourself.

5. **Cramming.** Last-minute learning doesn't build solid brain-links.

6. **Lazy learning.** Don't just practice easy material. That's like learning to play basketball by focusing on your dribbling. Use *deliberate practice*—focus on what you find most difficult.

7. **Ignoring your book.** If you are using a textbook in your studies, remember to take a picture walk through your book or course notes before you get going. And *be sure* to read about how to *do* problems before trying to *solve* problems!

8. **Not clearing up points of confusion.** Are there just a few points you don't get? Chances are, these are precisely the points that will be asked about on the test. Be sure to get help from your teacher or your friends.

9. **Distractions.** Choose somewhere you can focus when you study. It's often a good idea to leave your smartphone turned off and out of reach.

10. **Chatting with friends instead of studying with them.** Good study groups can be a great way to help you learn. But "study groups" that mostly gossip instead of study aren't much use.

Now You Try! *You* Become the Teacher

Terry, Al, and I have shared everything we can in this book to help you learn better. Now it is your turn.

Share something of what you've discovered through this book about learning. You can share with friends. Or a brother or sister. Or younger students at your school. (Younger kids love learning from older students.) You can even share with your parents and teachers. Tell them about Al's inspiring story in learning chemistry!

Share what you've learned—it's one of the best parts of learning!

Draw pictures. Make up funny stories. Talk about the memory palace technique. Explain what neurons and brain-links are and why they are important. Remember—everyone has struggles with their learning. If you've found ways to overcome these struggles, share them!

You'll remember the lessons better by teaching them. And you'll have fun while you're doing it. You get to become the teacher and help someone else at the same time!

Back to Santiago Ramón y Cajal

Santiago's research on neurons led him to an important discovery about the importance of geniuses—and the importance of more *seemingly* ordinary people.

Santiago admitted he wasn't a genius. So what was his magic? Why was he able to succeed and make great discoveries where even geniuses had failed? There are three important reasons.

First, Santiago kept his options open. His original passion was for *art*. And he never gave that up. He just added something new to his life when he decided to learn science. Gradually, science also became a passion for him. It is because Santiago developed abilities in two very different areas that he was able to win the Nobel Prize. He found a way to *keep* his beloved art, and he *applied it* to his science.[1]

So, as you grow up, be like Santiago. Don't narrow your options too much. The world is getting more complicated now. We need people with broader interests and skills. It's good to learn one topic deeply. But try to broaden your passions. If you are more of a math person, learn about art, music, and literature. If you are more artistic, musical, or literary, learn some math and science! You don't have to become a superstar. You just want to open doors that could help you in the future. It's worth repeating—you never know when your learning might come in handy.

The world needs people who combine talents from very different areas!

Second, Santiago was *persistent—he stuck with what he was trying to do.* When Santiago decided to begin learning math, he went back to the basics and slowly worked his way upward. It was hard for him. But he just kept at it. When he decided he wanted to figure something out, he kept at it. Persistently. Persistence is one of the most important parts of learning. But remember that persistence doesn't mean working endlessly on something. It means that you keep *returning* to your work after diffuse mode breaks!

Third, Santiago was *flexible.* Super-smart learners can get too used to being right. It feels *nice* to be right, but that feeling can also be addictive.[2] Santiago saw that some super-smart learners jump to conclusions quickly. (They've got "race car" brains, after all.) But if their conclusions are wrong, it can be hard for them to admit it. They can even deliberately avoid discovering whether they are wrong. All this feels nicer than admitting they might be mistaken. They can fall into a "rut think" of rightness.

Santiago wasn't a genius. So he got a lot of practice correcting his mistakes. Later, when he became a scientist, he actively *looked* for ways to determine whether he was right or wrong. *When he was wrong, he changed his mind.* This was an important part of what allowed him to make the groundbreaking discoveries that won him the Nobel Prize.

We don't all need or want to win the Nobel Prize. But we can discover something valuable from Santiago's example. One of the most important parts of learning is to be able to admit mistakes and flexibly change your mind. If you can learn to do this, you have the potential to contribute more than even some of the most brilliant of geniuses.

If, like most of us, you're not a genius, it's okay. You still have much to give to the world. No matter how smart you might be at the moment, you can use the strategies in this book to open new doors for yourself and for others.

Sometimes the learning journey can seem like a lonely one. But you're never alone. Using your mind's eye, you can see Terry, Al, and me striding on your mental mouse paths beside you, cheering you on as you learn. Our book showcases the work of the amazing research giants whose findings are doing so much to help you live a happier and more meaningful life, filled with the joys of discovery.

Terry, Al, and I wish you the very best of luck on your learning journey. And remember: Lady Luck favors the one who tries!

SOLUTIONS TO END-OF-CHAPTER PROBLEMS

CHAPTER 2: Easy Does It

1. To be in focused mode means you are paying close attention to something.

2. The diffuse mode is when your mind is wandering freely, not focusing on anything in particular. Your favorite diffuse mode activities are up to you!

3. A pinball machine helps you understand how your brain works. You can have two different types of tables. First, you can have a machine with the rubber bumpers spaced close together. This close-together layout mimics your tightly focused thinking when you are in focused mode. But you can have a different table with the bumpers spaced farther apart. This is like the diffuse mode, where your thoughts can range much more widely. If you don't keep your focus by using the flippers, the thought-ball can fall through a hole in the focused table onto the diffuse table!

4. Here are some other metaphors for focused and diffuse modes.[1]

In a soccer match:

- Looking like an umpire at the match is *focused* mode.
- Looking like a commentator at the match is *diffuse* mode.

On Google Maps:

- Zooming in is like *focused* mode.
- Zooming out is like *diffuse* mode.

  You need to toggle back and forth between zoomed in and zoomed out in order to find your way.

In a garden:

- *Focused* mode is like carefully spacing and planting the seeds in late winter.
- *Diffuse* mode is like spring, when the garden emerges with unexpected surprises due to the weather, birds, and insects.

5. The two ways you can get stuck in math and science problem solving. First, you haven't focused hard enough on the basics before starting to solve the problem. When this happens, you need to go back to your book or notes to get those basics in mind. Second, you *have* focused hard enough on the basics, but you haven't taken a break when you got stuck. Taking a break when you get stuck helps your diffuse mode to work in the background of your mind, while you're not aware of it.

6. The study habit you would change is up to you!

CHAPTER 3: I'll Do It Later, Honest!

1. Procrastination means delaying or postponing something that you should be doing.

2. Procrastination is bad for your learning because you run out of time to learn properly. And you spend energy worrying about it. That's a lose-lose situation.

3. Thinking about something you don't like or don't want to do fires up the insular cortex. This causes a painful feeling. To get rid of the painful feeling, we can end up switching our attention to something more pleasant. The pain in our brain goes away immediately—but we've just procrastinated.

4. This explanation is up to you!

5. The *reward* is the most important part of the Pomodoro process.

6. During the break between Pomodoros, try to do something that uses a different part of your brain. If you've just been *writing* a report, don't *write* a post on social media. The best breaks involve getting up and moving around.

7. If you happen to finish a task during the Pomodoro session, fine. But the point of the Pomodoro isn't to *finish* the task. It's just to work as intently as you can for 25 minutes.

8. Zombie mode is a great energy saver. It can be a bad use of your brainpower to think about every single thing.

9. Although zombie mode can help save energy, you can also find yourself falling into bad habits. Like doing something more pleasant instead of something that needs to be done. In other words, zombie mode can lead to procrastination.

10. The arsenic eaters got used to eating arsenic, and didn't realize it was harming them. In a similar way, we can get used to procrastinating, and not realize how much it is harming us.

11. *Active recall* means pulling key information from your own mind, instead of looking at your book or notes. One way to recall is to read a page, then look away and see if you can recall the key idea on that page.

CHAPTER 4: Brain-Links and Fun with Space Aliens

1. The <u>signals</u> that neurons send to other neurons form your <u>thoughts</u>.

2. This one's up to you.

3. The axon shocks the dendritic spine. In other words, a signal passes from the axon of one neuron to the dendritic spine of the next neuron.

4. When a metaphor breaks down and doesn't work anymore, you get a new one.

5. Microscopes back in the early 1900s weren't very good compared to what we can see today. Scientists thought your brain was one big interconnected network because the neurons came so close to one another that they couldn't see the tiny gap—the synaptic gap—in between them.

6. A set of brain-links are neurons that have become connected through repeated use of synaptic links. Brain-links are what develop when you learn something new and you practice repeatedly with it.

7. Mice run along forest paths, just like thoughts run along neurons and synapses. The more the mouse runs along the path, the deeper and wider the path gets. In a similar way, the more you think a thought, the thicker and wider the neural pathway becomes, and the stronger the brain-links become.

8. When you learn something new, you form a new set of <u>links/ synapses/dendritic spines</u> in your brain. (Any of these answers works.)

CHAPTER 6: Learning While You Sleep

1. Sleep is important when it comes to learning because that's when new dendritic spines and their synapse links really "pop" and grow larger. Sleep is also when the mind rehearses the information you've been learning. The electrical signals that arise while rehearsing during sleep are part of why the dendritic spines and their synapse links grow so rapidly.

2. Dendritic spines are like lie detectors because new spines and their synapses grow only if you're really focusing on the new information you want to learn—they can tell when you're not actually focusing!

3. When you practice a new idea, the synapse involved becomes stronger.

4. When you space out your learning over a number of days, you have more time to grow dendritic spines and their synaptic connections. Your neural architecture becomes stronger.

5. Give it a try!

6. This one's up to you!

CHAPTER 7: School Bags, Lockers, and Your Attentional Octopus

1. Your working memory is like a school bag because it's close at hand but can hold only a limited amount of information.

2. Your attentional octopus (your working memory) "lives" in your prefrontal cortex.

3. People's working memory can usually hold about four items of information. However, some people can hold more than four items, and some less.

4. Your long-term memory is like a locker because it can hold more "stuff." In fact, it can hold so much stuff that it can sometimes be hard to find a paticular item!

5. Your long-term memory is scattered around in different areas of your brain.

CHAPTER 8: Slick Tricks to Build Your Memory

1. It's definitely possible to develop a better long-term memory. (We don't know how to improve short-term memory, at present, anyway.) To improve your long-term memory, you can use Nelson Dellis's five memory tips (*focus, practice, picture, store,* and *recall*). You can also use the memory palace technique, songs, metaphors, note taking, teaching others, or putting yourself in the shoes of something you're trying to remember or understand.

2. The memory palace technique means imagining a place you know well, like your home, your route to school, or a map of your town, state, or country. Then you make memorable images involving the facts you are trying to remember. Next, deposit them at familiar places in your memory palace. Finally, practice recalling the images and what they represent.

3. We store information in two ways in long-term memory. *Facts* are hard to store. *Pictures* are easy to store.

4. To make an image stick even better in memory, make the image something wacky and memorable. And add some movement. *King Kong doing the hula on top of a* **pot** might help you remember that the letter *K* is the abbreviation for the element called ***potassium***.

CHAPTER 9: Why Brain-Links Are Important

1. Brain-links are important because they allow you to process information more quickly. Your attentional octopus doesn't need to do all the work.

2. Your "attentional octopus" is a metaphor for your attentional and working memory systems. It has only four arms, so it can hold only a limited amount of information. It can reach into long-term memory and bring information from there directly to working memory.

3. Getting dressed is a good example of a brain-linked procedure. When you first were learning how to dress on your own, it sometimes took five minutes or more. (Oops—the shirt's inside out and backwards!) Now that you've "linked" how to dress, it often takes only a minute.

   You may know an algebra problem inside and out, so you can actively recall every step. You can probably think of many more examples of skills, techniques, and concepts you have linked in sports, handicrafts, math, science, dance, language, and many other areas. Even just the simple ability to recognize the letter "a" is a set of links—recognizing the word "cat" is a bigger set of links.

4. The television, or other background noise, can distract your attentional octopus. This takes up one or more of its arms, making it more difficult for you to make full use of your working memory.

5. You should avoid task switching because it causes a lot of extra unnecessary work for your attentional octopus. For example, your octopus might be working with one set of brain-links. Then it has to switch to another set of brain-links. Then back to the first set. This kind of thing is tiring!

6. You can set your phone where you cannot see it when you are working on homework. If you are constantly glancing at your phone, you are dropping your brain-links, and you'll have to pick them up again. Another thing you can do is make friends with your phone by using an app on it to help you do a Pomodoro.

7. No, just understanding a concept is not enough to create a set of brain-links. You must practice the new concept to create the set of links. Understanding and practice go together. The more you practice, the more you understand what you are learning.

8. You become an expert in anything by developing a library of brain-links.

9. If I were being rescued from a fire, I would choose a firefighter who had physically practiced rescuing people from a burning building. Firefighting is a dangerous activity, where every second counts. The firefighter needs to be able to react quickly and appropriately to the danger that is swirling around. The firefighter needs well-practiced sets of brain-links that he or she can call on even under conditions of high stress. Such sets of links do not develop by simply watching.

CHAPTER 11: How to Pump Up Your Brain

1. The hippocampus is especially important in helping you remember facts and events.

2. Your brain is like a basketball team because new players arrive every year, while the older ones leave. The new players can learn new plays. Similarly, new neurons are born in the hippocampus every day, and they help you learn "new plays."

3. When BDNF is added to the brain, the <u>dendritic</u> <u>spines</u> grow tall and broad.

4. Exercise does the following:
   - **Helps your brain to produce BDNF**, which is like a fertilizer that helps your neurons grow.
   - **Improves your understanding, decision-making, and ability to focus.**
   - Helps you to **switch between tasks.**
   - Helps people to **recover** from mental illness.
   - **Releases chemicals that help you get new ideas.**

5. Vegetables from the onion and cabbage families, fruits of all colors, dark chocolate, and nuts are great choices for a healthy diet.

CHAPTER 12: Making Brain-Links

1. A puzzle is a good metaphor for the way we piece together concepts because each puzzle piece is like a set of brain-links.

Practicing with that set of brain-links brings out the color on the puzzle piece. When we put together enough puzzle pieces (brain-links), we've become an expert!

2. Interleaving is like randomly shuffling a deck of cards. Shuffling the deck means *any* card can come your way. If you practice a subject by interleaving, you'll be prepared for anything that comes your way. This helps you be better prepared for the unexpected questions on tests.

3. Lazy learning is when you practice only what comes easily for you, or what you've already learned.

4. Superman would say I'm never going to be able to take any mighty leaps with my learning!

5. The special advice to help with studying math, science, and other abstract subjects is this. First, find a problem. Then work that problem *yourself* enough times that it flows like a song through your mind.

CHAPTER 13: Asking Yourself Important Questions

1. Loud music with words is likely to be a distraction in your studies. But some people find that quiet music without words can help. Different people like different kinds of music when they are studying, and some people don't like music at all. It depends on you.

2. Your attentional octopus can become confused if you usually study in one place but then take a test in another place. If you are able to study in different places, you get used to latching onto your brain-links wherever you are.

3. If you think you learn only by listening ("auditory"), you can end up avoiding other means of learning, such as visualizing. This can cause your overall learning to suffer. The reality is everybody learns best by using as many of their senses as they can.

4. You can *see* an equation. You can read the equation out loud. This way, you can *hear* it and also *feel* the sounds as you make them in your mouth. Try extending your hands out on each side of you and imagining that one side of the equation is on

one hand, and the other side of the equation is on the other. (How does it feel? Is the equation "balanced"?) See if you can imagine physical meaning for the mathematical symbols. For example, sometimes a multiplication sign is like pushing. So if you multiply by a bigger number, you are pushing harder!

5. When you go to sleep, your brain cells shrink. This allows cerebral fluids to wash away toxins in the brain.

6. "Eat your frogs first" means trying to do the most difficult things first. This gives you the time to switch to other subjects temporarily if you get stuck and need a creative boost from the diffuse mode.

7. Plan on a firm quitting time for your studying. This will help you to concentrate more effectively when you are studying.

CHAPTER 14: Learning Surprises

1. *Action* and *spatial* video games help improve your thinking. Action video games help improve your ability to focus, and your vision. Spatial video games improve your ability to rotate objects in your mind's eye.

2. The bad aspect of video games is that they can be addictive. So they should be used in moderation.

3. The basic idea of note taking is to pick out key points from what you've heard so that you can review and strengthen brain-links. The best way to do this is to write by hand. Divide a sheet of paper into two parts, so you can take initial notes on one side and later make briefer notes on the other as you review and actively recall the key points.

4. "Rut think" means that your mind gets so used to running along certain mental pathways that it becomes stuck in a rut. You become less flexible in your thinking.

5. To be more creative and get better at something you are passionate about, you should spend a little time doing something very different. This helps keep you mentally flexible and more creative. Using metaphor, you can bring ideas from one subject to another subject—even if the subjects are very different!

6. *Transfer* is the ability to take an idea you've learned in one subject and use it to help you learn another subject. Metaphors can help with this process.

7. A poor working memory means that you don't have as many arms on your attentional octopus. So it's hard to hold complicated ideas in mind. You have to link some of the ideas in order to work with them. But the process of linking simplifies what you know! This can allow you to see simple and elegant insights and solutions that others can miss. Also, some thoughts easily slip out of the arms of your attentional octopus. But when some thoughts slip away, others slip in. This helps you to be more creative. Do you have to work harder than other people to learn and link information? Yes. But it's a great trade-off!

8. Many skills and subjects can be learned well, whether you learn them quickly or slowly. For example, it may take you longer to learn to ride a bicycle than another person, but you can still learn to ride a bicycle well. It may take you longer to learn to multiply, but you can still do multiplication. You may have to study twice as long (or more) to memorize the parts of a plant, but you can still memorize the parts of the plant.

CHAPTER 15: How to Do Well on Tests

1. The most important step before a test is to make sure you get a good night's sleep!

2. In the hard-start technique, you should leave a difficult problem when you are stuck and begin to grow frustrated.

3. When you feel panic rising before a test, practice deep breathing from the belly. Also, shift your thinking from "This test has made me afraid" to "This test has got me excited to do my best!"

4. To catch wrong answers on a test, blink, shift your attention, and then double-check your answers using a big-picture perspective. Ask yourself, "Does this really make sense?" Try to review the problems in a different order from when you first completed them.

SUGGESTED RESOURCES

Here are some worthwhile resources that can give a new perspective on many of the topics we've covered in this book.

Web Resources

> **Khan Academy.** This is a terrific resource. The more active practice you do after watching each video, the better! https://www.khanacademy.org

> **Smartick.** This program provides a solid foundation in mathematics built on sound practice. If you are struggling with mathematics, this is a great resource. If you are doing well in math, this resource will help you do even better. https://www.smartickmethod.com

> **BrainHQ.** One of the few "cognitive improvement" programs that has good science to back up their claims—particularly good for aging adults to help improve their concentration and focus. If your grandma or grandpa is complaining that they aren't as sharp as they used to be, this program's for them! https://www.brainhq.com/

> **Frontiers for Young Minds.** Science for kids, edited by kids, an open-access scientific journal written by scientists and

reviewed by a board of kids and teens. https://kids.frontiersin
.org/

> **The Queensland Brain Institute**, This Institute has excellent features, podcast, and a magazine. https://qbi.uq.edu.au/

> **BrainFacts.org**. An excellent website with all sorts of information about how your brain works. http://www.brainfacts
.org/

> **The Nervous System, Crash Course**. https://www.youtube
.com/watch?time_continue=113&v=qPix_X-9t7E. This is funny
as well as informative.

> **"5 Memory Tips to Get You Started,"** by Nelson Dellis. Four-time US Memory Champion Nelson Dellis has a wonderful series of memory tip videos—this is a good one to help you get started. https://www.youtube.com/watch?v=bEx60e
_45-Q. See also Nelson's book *Remember It!* on p. 219.

> **"Learning How to Learn: Powerful Mental Tools to Help You Master Tough Subjects,"** a massive open online course by Barb Oakley and Terrence Sejnowski through University of California, San Diego. https://www.coursera.org/learn/
learning-how-to-learn.

> **"Mindshift: Break Through Obstacles to Learning and Discover Your Hidden Potential,"** a massive open online course by Barb Oakley and Terrence Sejnowski through University of California, San Diego. https://www.coursera.org/
learn/mindshift.

Books for Young Adults About the Brain

> *My First Book About the Brain*, by Patricia J. Wynne and Donald M. Silver (New York: Dover Children's Science Books, 2013), 32 pages. This award-winning coloring book is so informative that it is used in some regular classes. Suitable for ages 8–12, but grown-ups also seem to enjoy the relaxing process of coloring while they learn.

> *The Brain: All About Our Nervous System and More!*, by Seymour Simon (New York: HarperCollins, 2006), 32 pages, for ages 6–10. Features color images taken with radiological

scanners, discussions of long- and short-term memory, neurons, dendrites, and more.

> *What Goes On in My Head?*, by Robert Winston (New York: DK Publishing, 2014), 96 pages, for ages 9–13. A colorful book that "helps you wrap your head around how the brain works."

Top Neuroscience-Based Programs for People with Learning Disabilities

including struggling readers and people with dyslexia, auditory processing disorder, autism spectrum disorder, and more general learning disabilities

> https://www.scilearn.com, in particular, their "Fast ForWord" and "Reading Assistant" software.

Neuroscience-Based Program for English Language Learners

> https://www.scilearn.com, in particular, their "Reading Assistant" software. (There are many programs and centers around the world.)

Books for Adults About Learning

> *The Art of Changing the Brain: Enriching the Practice of Teaching by Exploring the Biology of Learning*, by James E. Zull (Sterling, VA: Stylus Publishing, 2002).

> *The Art of Learning: An Inner Journey to Optimal Performance*, by Josh Waitzkin (New York: Free Press, 2008).

> *Deep Work: Rules for Focused Success in a Distracted World*, by Cal Newport (New York: Grand Central Publishing, 2016). Learning often involves being able to focus intently, and Cal's book gives great ideas along those lines.

> *I Am Gifted, So Are You!,* by Adam Khoo (Singapore: Marshall Cavendish, 2014). We love Adam's personal story and practical insights.
> *Make It Stick: The Science of Successful Learning,* by Peter C. Brown, Henry L. Roediger III, and Mark A. McDaniel (Cambridge, MA: Harvard University Press, 2014). One of our very favorite books on learning for adults.
> *A Mind for Numbers: How to Succeed in Math and Science (Even If You Flunked Algebra)* by Barbara Oakley (New York: Tarcher/ Penguin, 2014). Even if we do say so ourselves, this is actually a great general book on learning—it relates some of the ideas of *Learning How to Learn* but from an adult prospective that includes many additional insights.
> *Mindshift: Break Through Obstacles to Learning and Discover Your Hidden Potential,* by Barbara Oakley (New York: TarcherPerigee, 2017). This book explores how you can change yourself through learning—sometimes more than you might think!
> *Peak: Secrets from the New Science of Expertise,* by Anders Ericsson and Robert Pool (New York: Eamon Dolan/Houghton Mifflin Harcourt, 2016). Incidentally, what Anders calls a "mental representation" is analogous to what we in *Learning How to Learn* call a "set of brain-links."
> *Remember It! The Names of People You Meet, All Your Passwords, Where You Left Your Keys, and Everything Else You Tend to Forget* by Nelson Dellis (New York: Abrams Image, 2018). One of the best books on memory development for adults.

ILLUSTRATION CREDITS

59 Santiago Ramón y Cajal in Zaragoza, Spain (ca. 1870), https://commons.wikimedia.org/wiki/File:Santiago_Ram%C3%B3n_y_Cajal,_estudiante_de_medicina_en_Zaragoza_1876.jpg.

69 Alistair McConville as a boy, photo courtesy Alistair McConville.

70 Alistair McConville with students, photo by Sarah Sheldrake, courtesy Alistair McConville.

71 Alistair McConville with Violet, photo by Sarah Sheldrake, courtesy Alistair McConville.

76 Photo of Guang Yang, courtesy Guang Yang and NYU Langone Health.

77 Inverted light microscopy image of neuron altered from original image, courtesy Guang Yang.

80 Image credit: modified from patellar tendon reflex arc by Amiya Sarkar (CC BY-SA 4.0); the modified image is licensed under a CC BY-SA 4.0 license, obtained from https://www.khanacademy.org/science/biology/behavioral-biology/animal-behavior/a/innate-behaviors.

81 Brick walls, © 2014 Kevin Mendez

83 Iliriana Baftiu using recall, © 2018 Bafti Baftiu.

91 Puzzle of man's face, © 2014 Kevin Mendez.

97 Photo of Nelson Dellis, courtesy Nelson Dellis.

106 Monkeys in a benzene ring formation, from *Berichte der Durstigen Chemischen Gesellschaft* (1886), p. 3536.

106 Conventional benzene ring modified from http://en.wikipedia.org/wiki/File: Benzene-2D-full.svg.

108 Tom Morris, https://en.wikipedia.org/wiki/Rubber_duck_debugging#/media/File:Rubber_duck_assisting_with_debugging.jpg.

112 Rachel Oakley learning to back up a car, © 2018 Philip Oakley.

118 Rachel easily backing up, © 2018 Philip Oakley.

127 Terry with members of the radio club, photo courtesy Terrence Sejnowski.

128 Terry and fellow club members adjusting a radio antenna, photo courtesy Terrence Sejnowski.

129 Terry at Princeton, photo courtesy Terrence Sejnowski.

130 Terry today at the Salk Institute, © 2014 Philip Oakley.

134 Julius Yego, photo by Erik van Leeuwen, attribution: Erik van Leeuwen (bron: Wikipedia).—erki.nl, GFDL, https://commons.wikimedia.org/w/index.php?curid=42666617.

135 Https://commons.wikimedia.org/wiki/File:Hippocampus_and_seahorse_cropped.JPG.

137 Image of "BDNF-based synaptic repair" by kind permission of Bai Lu, after "BDNF-based synaptic repair as a disease-modifying strategy for neurodegenerative diseases," *Nature Reviews Neuroscience* 14, 401–416 (2013).

145 Puzzle of man in Mustang, partly assembled, image © 2014 Kevin Mendez and Philip Oakley.

145 Puzzle of man in Mustang, mostly assembled, image © 2014 Kevin Mendez and Philip Oakley.

145 Puzzle of man in Mustang, faint and partly assembled, image © 2014 Kevin Mendez and Philip Oakley.

152 Benjamin Franklin, by Joseph Siffred Duplessis, National Portrait Gallery, Smithsonian Institution, gift of the Morris and Gwendolyn Cafritz Foundation, http://npg.si.edu/object/npg_NPG.87.43.

155 Construction paper brain-links, ©2018 Zella McNichols.

176 Al enjoys a video game with his son, Jacob, photo by Sarah Sheldrake, courtesy Alistair McConville.

183 Elena Benito on a Segway, photo courtesy Elena Benito.

231 Dime solution, image courtesy the author.

All other illustrations by Oliver Young.

ACKNOWLEDGMENTS

We would like to thank Joanna Ng, our editor at Penguin. She is an extraordinary editor, and this project is far the better for it. Our literary agent, Rita Rosenkranz, has provided extraordinary support and guidance. Adam Johnson did a superb job with the cover design. Sheila Moody was a terrific copy editor, and Sabrina Bowers did the superlative layout. Our thanks as well to Marlena Brown and Roshe Anderson for their astute support in publicity and marketing.

We are grateful for the help of the following individuals. (We beg forgiveness of anyone whose name we might have inadvertently overlooked.)

Unas and Ahmed Aamir; Ben, Maureen, Cooper, and Crash Ackerly; Cathi Allen; Arden and Eileen Arabian; Bafti and Iliriana Baftiu; Maliha Balala; John Becker; Robert Bell; Elena Benito; Pamela Bet; Annie Brookman-Byrne; Keith Budge and Bedales School; Paul Burgmayer and students; Christina Buu-Hoan and Kailani and Gavin Buu-Doerr; Meigra and Keira Chin; Romilly Cocking; Ruth Collins; Christine Costa; Massimo Curatella; Andy Dalal; Simon and Nate Dawson; Yoni Dayan; Javier DeFelipe; Pablo Denis; Sudeep Dhillon; Melania Di Napoli; Matthieu Dondey; Catherine Dorgan and family; Susan Dreher; Dina Eltareb; Richard Felder; Jessica Finnigan and family; Shamim Formoso and students; Jeffrey Frankel; Beatrice Golomb; Jane Greiner; Maureen Griffin and students; Tarik Guenab; Gary Hafer; Greg Hammons; Paula Hoare; Richard Hypio; Shaju and Isabella Jacob; M. Johnson; Karine Joly and her sons Horatio and Valerius; Jonneke Jorissen; Kalyani Kandula; Sahana Katakol; Tanya and Laura Kirsch; Jake Kitzmann; Cristina Koppel; Barbora Kvapilová; Loi Laing; Aune Lillemets; Susan Lucci; Beate Luo; Jennifer and Matthew Mackerras; Genevieve Malcolm; Kyle Marcroft; Anaya, Nafisa, and Mohamed Marei; Max Markarian; David Matten; Susan Maurice and students; Jo, Lulu, Ewan, and Jacob McConville; Zella and Jeremiah McNichols; Jim Meador; Jill Meisenheimer; Gerry Montemayor; Mary Murphy; Aleksandra Nekrasova; Patricia Nester; Michael Nussbaum; Philip, Roslyn, and Rachel Oakley; Jennifer Padberg; Saadia Peerzada; Violeta Piasecka; Michael Pichel; Jocelyn Roberts; Rev. Dr. Melissa Rudolph; Dennis Ryan; Leslie Schneider; Grace Sherrill; Julia Shewry; Maya Sirton; Vince Stevenson; Ray Symmes; Jimi Taiwo; Lauren Teixeira; Louise Terry; Barbara Tremblay; Donna and Hannah Trenholm; Bonny Tsai; Bonnie Turnbull; Robert Van Til and Oakland University; Vickie Weiss and students; Alan Woodruff; Arthur Worsley; Julia Zanutta. And Violet (the dog).

REFERENCES

We're giving references to some of the most important material here so you can understand what good references look like. If you're hungry for more information, please see the far more complete references in Barb's books *A Mind for Numbers* (Tarcher/Penguin, 2014) and *Mindshift* (TarcherPerigee, 2017).

Anacker, C, and R Hen. "Adult hippocampal neurogenesis and cognitive flexibility linking memory and mood." *Nature Reviews: Neuroscience* 18, 6 (2017): 335–346.

Anderson, ML. *After Phrenology: Neural Reuse and the Interactive Brain.* Cambridge, MA: MIT Press, 2014.

Anguera, JA, et al. "Video game training enhances cognitive control in older adults." *Nature* 501, 7465 (2013): 97–101.

Baddeley, A, et al. *Memory.* New York: Psychology Press, 2009.

Bavelier, D, et al. "Brain plasticity through the life span: Learning to learn and action video games." *Annual Review of Neuroscience* 35 (2012): 391–416.

Beilock, S. *Choke: What the Secrets of the Brain Reveal about Getting It Right When You Have To.* New York: Free Press, 2010.

Belluck, P. "To really learn, quit studying and take a test." *New York Times,* January 20, 2011. http://www.nytimes.com/2011/01/21/science/21memory.html.

Bird, CM, et al. "Consolidation of complex events via reinstatement in posterior cingulate cortex." *Journal of Neuroscience* 35, 43 (2015): 14426–14434.

Bjork, EL, and RA Bjork. "Making things hard on yourself, but in a good way: Creating desirable difficulties to enhance learning." Chapter 5 in *Psychology and the Real World: Essays Illustrating Fundamental Contributions to Society*, MA Gernsbacher, RW Pew, LM Hough, and JR Pomerantz, eds. New York: Worth Publishers, 2011, pp. 59–68.

Brown, PC, et al. *Make It Stick: The Science of Successful Learning*. Cambridge MA: Harvard University Press, 2014.

Burton, R. *On Being Certain: Believing You Are Right Even When You're Not*. New York: St. Martin's Griffin, 2008.

Butler, AC. "Repeated testing produces superior transfer of learning relative to repeated studying." *Journal of Experimental Psychology: Learning, Memory, and Cognition* 36, 5 (2010): 1118.

Carpenter, SK, et al. "Using spacing to enhance diverse forms of learning: Review of recent research and implications for instruction." *Educational Psychology Review* 24, 3 (2012): 369–378.

Christoff, K, et al. "Mind-wandering as spontaneous thought: A dynamic framework." *Nature Reviews Neuroscience* 17, 11 (2016): 718–731.

Coffield, F. "Learning styles: Unreliable, invalid and impractical and yet still widely used." Chapter 13 in *Bad Education: Debunking Myths in Education*, P Adey and J Dillon, eds. Berkshire, UK: Open University Press, 2012, pp. 215–230.

Cowan, N. "The magical number 4 in short-term memory: A reconsideration of mental storage capacity." *Behavioral and Brain Sciences* 24, 1 (2001): 87–114.

DeCaro, MS, et al. "When higher working memory capacity hinders insight." *Journal of Experimental Psychology: Learning, Memory and Cognition* 42, 1 (2015): 39–49.

DeFelipe, J, et al. "The death of Cajal and the end of scientific romanticism and individualism." *Trends in Neurosciences* 37, 10 (2014): 525–527.

Di, X, and BB Biswal. "Modulatory interactions between the default mode network and task positive networks in resting-state." *Peer Journal* 2 (2014): e367.

Dresler, M, et al. "Mnemonic training reshapes brain networks to support superior memory." *Neuron* 93, 5 (2017): 1227–1235.e6.

Dunlosky, J, et al. "Improving students' learning with effective learning techniques: Promising directions from cognitive and educational psychology." *Psychological Science in the Public Interest* 14, 1 (2013): 4–58.

Dweck, CS. *Mindset: The New Psychology of Success*. New York: Random House, 2006.

Ericsson, KA. "Exceptional memorizers: Made, not born." *Trends in Cognitive Sciences* 7, 6 (2003): 233–235.

———. "The influence of experience and deliberate practice on the development of superior expert performance." *Cambridge Handbook of Expertise and Expert Performance* 38 (2006): 685–705.

Ericsson, KA, and R Pool. *Peak: Secrets from the New Science of Expertise.* New York: Eamon Dolan/Houghton Mifflin Harcourt, 2016.

Felder, RM. "Memo to students who have been disappointed with their test grades." *Chemical Engineering Education* 33, 2 (1999): 136–137.

Gallistel, CR, and LD Matzel. "The neuroscience of learning: Beyond the Hebbian synapse." *Annual Review of Psychology* 64, 1 (2013): 169–200.

Gobet, F, et al. "What's in a name? The multiple meanings of 'chunk' and 'chunking.'" *Frontiers in Psychology* 7 (2016): 102.

Guida, A, et al. "Functional cerebral reorganization: A signature of expertise? Reexamining Guida, Gobet, Tardieu, and Nicolas' (2012) two-stage framework." *Frontiers in Human Neuroscience* 7, doi: 10.3389/fnhum.2013.00590. eCollection (2013): 590.

Guida, A, et al. "How chunks, long-term working memory and templates offer a cognitive explanation for neuroimaging data on expertise acquisition: A two-stage framework." *Brain and Cognition* 79, 3 (2012): 221–244.

Guskey, TR. "Closing achievement gaps: Revisiting Benjamin S. Bloom's 'Learning for Mastery.'" *Journal of Advanced Academics* 19, 1 (2007): 8–31.

Hunt, A, and D Thomas. *The Pragmatic Programmer: From Journeyman to Master.* Reading, MA: Addison-Wesley Professional, 1999.

Karpicke, JD, and A Bauernschmidt. "Spaced retrieval: Absolute spacing enhances learning regardless of relative spacing." *Journal of Experimental Psychology: Learning, Memory, and Cognition* 37, 5 (2011): 1250.

Karpicke, JD, and JR Blunt. "Retrieval practice produces more learning than elaborative studying with concept mapping." *Science* 331, 6018 (2011): 772–775.

Kirschner, PA, et al. "Why minimal guidance during instruction does not work: An analysis of the failure of constructivist, discovery, problem-based, experiential, and inquiry-based teaching." *Educational Psychologist* 41, 2 (2006): 75–86.

Lin, T-W, and Y-M Kuo. "Exercise benefits brain function: The monoamine connection." *Brain Sciences* 3, 1 (2013): 39–53.

Lu, B, et al. "BDNF-based synaptic repair as a disease-modifying strategy for neurodegenerative diseases." *Nature Reviews: Neuroscience* 14, 6 (2013): 401.

Luksys, G, and C Sandi. "Synaptic mechanisms and cognitive computations underlying stress effects on cognitive function." Chapter 12 in *Synaptic Stress and Pathogenesis of Neuropsychiatric Disorders*, M Popoli, D Diamond, and G Sanacora, eds. New York: Springer, 2014, pp. 203–222.

Maguire, EA, et al. "Routes to remembering: The brains behind superior memory." *Nature Neuroscience* 6, 1 (2003): 90.

Moussa, M, et al. "Consistency of network modules in resting-state fMRI connectome data." *PLoS ONE* 7, 8 (2012): e44428.

Oakley, BA. *A Mind for Numbers: How to Excel at Math and Science.* New York: Tarcher/Penguin, 2014.

Oakley, BA. *Mindshift: Break Through Obstacles to Learning and Discover Your Hidden Potential.* New York: TarcherPerigee, 2017.

Partnoy, F. *Wait: The Art and Science of Delay.* New York: PublicAffairs, 2012.

Patston, LL, and LJ Tippett. "The effect of background music on cognitive performance in musicians and nonmusicians." *Music Perception: An Interdisciplinary Journal* 29, 2 (2011): 173–183.

Phillips, DC. "The good, the bad, and the ugly: The many faces of constructivism." *Educational Researcher* 24, 7 (1995): 5–12.

Qin, S, et al. "Hippocampal-neocortical functional reorganization underlies children's cognitive development." *Nature Neuroscience* 17 (2014): 1263–1269.

Ramón y Cajal, S. *Recollections of My Life.* Cambridge, MA: MIT Press, 1937 (reprint 1989). Originally published as *Recuerdos de Mi Vida* in Madrid, 1901–1917, translated by EH Craigie.

Rittle-Johnson, B, et al. "Not a one-way street: Bidirectional relations between procedural and conceptual knowledge of mathematics." *Educational Psychology Review* 27, 4 (2015): 587–597.

Roediger, HL, and MA Pyc. "Inexpensive techniques to improve education: Applying cognitive psychology to enhance educational practice." *Journal of Applied Research in Memory and Cognition* 1, 4 (2012): 242–248.

Rogowsky, BA, et al. "Matching learning style to instructional method: Effects on comprehension." *Journal of Educational Psychology* 107, 1 (2015): 64–78.

Rohrer, D, et al. "The benefit of interleaved mathematics practice is not limited to superficially similar kinds of problems." *Psychonomic Bulletin Review* (2014): 1323–1330.

Rohrer, D, and H Pashler. "Recent research on human learning challenges conventional instructional strategies." *Educational Researcher* 39, 5 (2010): 406–412.

Rupia, EJ, et al. "Fight-flight or freeze-hide? Personality and metabolic phenotype mediate physiological defence responses in flatfish." *Journal of Animal Ecology* 85, 4 (2016): 927–937.

Sapolsky, RM. "Stress and the brain: Individual variability and the inverted-U." *Nature Neuroscience* 18, 10 (2015): 1344–1346.

Schenk, S, et al. "Games people play: How video games improve probabilistic learning." *Behavioural Brain Research* 335, Supplement C (2017): 208–214.

Scullin, MK, et al. "The effects of bedtime writing on difficulty falling asleep: A polysomnographic study comparing to-do lists and completed activity lists." *Journal of Experimental Psychology: General* 147, 1 (2018): 139.

Settles, B, and Hagiwara, M. "The best time of day to learn a new language, according to Duolingo data," *Quartz*, Feb 26, 2018. https://qz.com/1215361/the-best-time-of-day-to-learn-a-new-language-according-duolingo-data.

Shenhav, A, et al. "Toward a rational and mechanistic account of mental effort." *Annual Review of Neuroscience* 40, 1 (2017): 99–124.

Shih, Y-N, et al. "Background music: Effects on attention performance." *Work* 42, 4 (2012): 573–578.

Smith, AM, et al. "Retrieval practice protects memory against acute stress." *Science* 354, 6315 (2016).

Sweller, J, et al. *Cognitive Load Theory.* New York: Springer, 2011.

Szuhany, KL, et al. "A meta-analytic review of the effects of exercise on brain-derived neurotrophic factor." *Journal of Psychiatric Research* 60 (2015): 56–64.

Thompson, WF, et al. "Fast and loud background music disrupts reading comprehension." *Psychology of Music* 40, 6 (2012): 700–708.

Thurston, WP. "Mathematical education." *Notices of the American Mathematical Society* 37, 7 (1990): 844–850.

van der Schuur, WA, et al. "The consequences of media multitasking for youth: A review." *Computers in Human Behavior* 53 (2015): 204–215.

Van Praag, H. "Exercise and the brain: Something to chew on." *Trends in Neurosciences* 32, 5 (2009): 283–290.

Van Praag, H, et al. "Running enhances neurogenesis, learning, and long-term potentiation in mice." *Proceedings of the National Academy of Sciences of the United States of America* 96, 23 (1999): 13427–13431.

Vlach, HA, and CM Sandhofer. "Distributing learning over time: The spacing effect in children's acquisition and generalization of science concepts." *Child Development* 83, 4 (2012): 1137–1144.

Waitzkin, J. *The Art of Learning: An Inner Journey to Optimal Performance.* New York: Free Press, 2008.

Walker, M. *Why We Sleep: Unlocking the Power of Sleep and Dreams.* New York: Scribner, 2017.

White, HA, and P Shah. "Creative style and achievement in adults with attention-deficit/hyperactivity disorder." *Personality and Individual Differences* 50, 5 (2011): 673–677.

Willingham, D. *Why Don't Students Like School? A Cognitive Scientist Answers Questions About How the Mind Works and What It Means for the Classroom.* San Francisco, CA: Jossey-Bass, 2010.

Xie, L, et al. "Sleep drives metabolite clearance from the adult brain." *Science* 342, 6156 (2013): 373–377.

Yang, G, et al. "Sleep promotes branch-specific formation of dendritic spines after learning." *Science* 344, 6188 (2014): 1173–1178.

Zull, JE. *The Art of Changing the Brain: Enriching the Practice of Teaching by Exploring the Biology of Learning.* Sterling, VA: Stylus Publishing, 2002.

NOTES

CHAPTER 2: Easy Does It

1 Congratulations for visiting us here at the end of the book! This is the first endnote. Most of these endnotes are for more mature readers who might be interested in tracking down the source of some of the ideas we're presenting in this book. We can't give every source—the endnotes would then be much larger than the rest of the book. But we can give some of what we think are the more important and interesting sources. Well-researched books usually have endnotes, so you can check for yourself whether the research behind the book is worthwhile. Endnotes also give other information that the author of a book finds interesting, but is kind of a side topic. Sometimes it's a bit of a toss-up whether to put something in a footnote or an endnote. Do not worry if you find yourself skipping the endnotes.

This first endnote in our book gives more information about the focused mode. Cognitive psychologists call the small networks of the focused mode "task positive networks." Two scientists named Xin Di and Bharat B. Biswal published a paper about this concept in 2014. I'll refer to this paper in a shorthand way as "Di and Biswal, 2014." You can find more complete information about that paper in the list of references.

What we call "diffuse" mode in this book is thought of by neuroscientists in different ways. Sometimes researchers think of this mode as consisting of many different neural resting states (Moussa et al., 2012). At other times, they think of this mode as alternate different forms of the "default mode network." See the paper by Kalina Christoff and her coauthors listed in the

References section for a great review of the different parts of the brain used when the brain is relaxing (Christoff et al., 2016). (Note that we often use "et al." to mean the list of all remaining authors.) Warning: Christoff's paper, like many of the papers we recommend in the endnotes, is pretty advanced.

2 With appreciation to Joanna Łukasiak-Hołysz.

3 https://www.famousscientists.org/7-great-examples-of-scientific -discoveries-made-in-dreams/.

4 Just move the coins as shown—do you see how the new triangle will point down?

CHAPTER 3: I'll Do It Later, Honest!

1 Karpicke and Blunt, 2011; Bird et al., 2015.

2 Smith et al., 2016. Note that what we are calling "active recall" is typically referred to as "retrieval practice" in the literature.

3 Karpicke and Blunt, 2011.

CHAPTER 4: Brain-Links and Fun with Space Aliens

1 Ramón y Cajal, 1937 (reprint 1989).

2 Yes, we know there are neurotransmitters involved. But we'd rather avoid taking things to a deeper level of complexity.

3 People often say this phrase was first used in 1949 by Donald Hebb, a Canadian neuropsychologist. But this phrase is just a quick way of summarizing one of Hebb's key ideas. Hebb's theory is more complex, as any neuroscientist would be happy to tell you.

4 In our book, we'll use the phrase "set of brain-links." We call the process of creating a set of brain-links *linking*. Neuroscientists

instead use the terms *chunk* and *chunking* (see Guida et al., 2013; Guida et al., 2012). Cognitive psychologists use the term *mental representation* for a similar concept (see Ericsson and Pool, 2016). We're choosing to use the term *brain-links* because the term *chunk*, although well established in neuroscience, can be confusing. (See Gobet et al., 2016, for a discussion of the confusion.) *Mental representation*, on the other hand, doesn't provide that sense of the connectivity of neurons that is provided by the term *brain-links*.

5 Anacker and Hen, 2017.

6 Learning also appears to spur the creation of new neurons. The birth and growth of new neurons is called "neurogenesis." This is a very hot area in today's neuroscience and researchers have a lot to learn. See Anacker and Hen, 2017.

   I'd like to remind readers that we're painting a simple picture of important processes. There are many other processes involved in learning and memory. See, for example, Gallistel and Matzel, 2013.

7 The more you practice, the stronger your brain-links get. The actual processes are a lot more complex than what we're showing here with the symbolic doubled pair of neurons in the set of brain-links. In reality, the connectivity of individual synapses increases; more synapses and neurons can join the set of links; a process called myelination ("MILE-en-nation") occurs that insulates and helps speed up the signals; and many other processes unfold.

8 Anderson, 2014.

9 Being wise is more important than money. Life is like a play: Each person plays a different role and is, to some extent, performing.

10 With thanks to Elena Benito for the ideas of this section (email correspondence, November 2017).

CHAPTER 6: Learning While You Sleep

1 Yang et al., 2014.

2 Carpenter et al., 2012; Vlach and Sandhofer, 2012.

3 Karpicke and Bauernschmidt, 2011.

CHAPTER 7: School Bags, Lockers, and Your Attentional Octopus

1 One of the best research-oriented books about memory is Baddeley et al., 2009.

2 Cowan, 2001. So technically, we've got a quadrapus here.

3 Qin et al., 2014.

4 Anguera et al., 2013.

CHAPTER 8: Slick Tricks to Build Your Memory

1 We put this note in for more advanced learners who might have a better sense of the brain. You might be wondering what the real difference is biologically between semantic and episodic memory. As best as we can tell you now, it looks like semantic memory is associated with the frontal and temporal cortexes, while episodic memory is associated, at least initially, with the hippocampus. But there's a lot of work to be done yet in understanding memory!

2 You can also find these tips on Nelson's YouTube video: https://www.youtube.com/watch?v=bEx60e_45-Q.

3 Ericsson, 2003; Maguire et al., 2003; Dresler et al., 2017.

4 Hunt and Thomas, 1999, p. 95.

5 Correspondence from Nelson Dellis to Barb Oakley, September 2, 2017.

CHAPTER 9: Why Brain-Links Are Important

1 In an earlier chapter, we mentioned that what we're calling a *set of brain-links* is what neuroscientists sometimes call *neural chunks* and cognitive psychologists call *mental representations*.

2 Long-term memories are latent in the anatomical organization of the brain's many different networks. Sensory inputs, or inputs from other brain areas, can activate a subset of the neurons, electrically and biochemically. So when we say "link," we actually mean "activation."

3 Rittle-Johnson et al., 2015.

4 See *A Mind for Numbers*, beginning on page 184, along with the accompanying endnotes, for a more detailed discussion of this area.

5 Partnoy, 2012, p. 73. Partnoy goes on to note: "Sometimes having an understanding of precisely what we are doing unconsciously can kill the natural spontaneity. If we are too self-conscious, we will impede our instincts when we need them. Yet if we aren't self-conscious at all, we will never improve on our instincts. The challenge during a period of seconds is to be aware of the factors that go into our decisions . . . but not to be so aware of them that they are stilted and ineffectual" (p. 111).

6 Guskey, 2007.

7 Sweller et al., 2011.

8   Shenhav et al., 2017; van der Schuur et al., 2015.

9   With thanks to Elena Benito for the ideas of this section (email correspondence, November 2017).

CHAPTER 11: How to Pump Up Your Brain

1   Van Praag et al., 1999.

2   Szuhany et al., 2015.

3   Lu et al., 2013.

4   Van Praag, 2009.

5   Lin and Kuo, 2013.

CHAPTER 12: Making Brain-Links

1   Thurston, 1990, pp. 846–847.

2   Ericsson, 2006.

3   Butler, 2010. Two great papers that cover study methods that seem to work the best for students are Roediger and Pyc, 2012, and Dunlosky et al., 2013. Adult-level books that cover recent research about learning and how to apply it in your life are Brown et al., 2014, and of course Oakley, 2014, and Oakley, 2017. Robert and Elizabeth Bjork's work on "desirable difficulties" is also relevant here—for an overview, see Bjork and Bjork, 2011.

4   Rohrer and Pashler, 2010; Rohrer et al., 2014.

5   Phillips, 1995; Kirschner et al., 2006.

6   Rittle-Johnson et al., 2015.

7   With thanks for this idea to Zella McNichols (email correspondence, Jeremiah McNichols, December 7, 2017).

CHAPTER 13: Asking Yourself Important Questions

1   Baddeley et al., 2009, chapter 8.

2   Some of the information in this section is taken from Barb's video in the Mindshift MOOC: https://www.coursera.org/learn /mindshift/lecture/K0N78/2-9-integrate-all-your-senses-into -learning-the-pitfalls-of-learning-styles. See Beth Rogowsky's research at Rogowsky et al., 2015. See also Beth's webinar with Terry: http://www.brainfacts.org/sensing-thinking-behaving /learning-and-memory/articles/2016/learning-styles-hurt -learning-101216/. In this webinar, Beth makes the important point that teachers who make a point of emphasizing "teaching to the right learning style" can be setting themselves up to be

sued. Other resources include Coffield, 2012, and the excellent discussion in Willingham, 2010.

3 Xie et al., 2013.

4 Walker, 2017.

5 Along these lines, one recent study (Settles and Hagiwara, 2018) showed that the best learners on the language-learning app Duolingo were the ones who reviewed right before bedtime every night, including weekends.

6 Patston and Tippett, 2011; Shih et al., 2012; Thompson et al., 2012.

7 With appreciation to Kalyani Kandula (email correspondence, November 22, 2017).

CHAPTER 14: Learning Surprises

1 Bavelier et al., 2012; Anguera et al., 2013; Schenk et al., 2017.

2 DeCaro et al., 2015.

3 White and Shah, 2011.

CHAPTER 15: How to Do Well on Tests

1 Belluck, 2011; Karpicke and Blunt, 2011.

2 Visit Dr. Felder's website at http://www4.ncsu.edu/unity/lockers/users/f/felder/public/ for an enormous assortment of useful information on learning in the STEM disciplines. His original test checklist can be found at Felder, 1999.

3 Smith et al., 2016.

4 Sapolsky, 2015; Luksys and Sandi, 2014.

5 Beilock, 2010, pp. 140–141.

6 Rupia et al., 2016.

CHAPTER 16: Going from "Have to" to "Get to"

1 DeFelipe et al., 2014.

2 Burton, 2008.

SOLUTIONS TO END-OF-CHAPTER PROBLEMS

1 Metaphors thanks to commentators Vikrant Karandikar, Juan Fran Gómez Martín, and Dennise Cepeda on the Mindshift MOOC.

INDEX

Page numbers with an *n* refer to notes at the bottom of the page.

ABOUT THE AUTHORS AND ILLUSTRATOR

Dr. Barbara Oakley is the bestselling author of *Mindshift* and *A Mind for Numbers*, which has been translated into more than a dozen languages. With Terrence Sejnowski, she co-created and teaches the massive online open course "Learning How to Learn: Powerful Mental Tools to Help You Master Tough Subjects." It is the world's most popular massive open online course, with millions of students. Oakley has been profiled in the *New York Times* and the *Wall Street Journal*, among other publications.

She speaks widely at corporations, universities, and a broad spectrum of associations and institutions. Her insightful and engaging keynote lectures and seminars on effective learning and effective teaching have been presented in dozens of countries. As the Ramón y Cajal Distinguished Scholar of Global Digital Learning at McMaster University, she consults and conducts workshops worldwide on making effective online teaching materials.

Oakley is also a Fellow of the Institute of Electrical and Electronic Engineers (IEEE), Michigan's Distinguished Professor of the Year, and Professor of Engineering at Oakland University in

Rochester, Michigan. Her research and interests have led her to both neuroscience and MOOC-making. Her focus is on improving education around the world by providing practical insights grounded on neuroscientific research. She has won some of engineering's top teaching awards, including the American Society of Engineering Education Chester F. Carlson Award for outstanding technical innovation in STEM pedagogy and the Theo L. Pilkington Award for exemplary work in bioengineering education. Learn more about her work at barbaraoakley.com.

Dr. Terrence (Terry) Joseph Sejnowski is an Investigator at the Howard Hughes Medical Institute, and Francis Crick Professor at the Salk Institute for Biological Studies, where he directs the Computational Neurobiology Laboratory. In 2004, he was named the Francis Crick Professor and the Director of the Crick-Jacobs Center for Theoretical and Computational Biology at the Salk Institute. Sejnowski is also Professor of Biological Sciences and Adjunct Professor in the Departments of Neurosciences, Psychology, Cognitive Science, Computer Science, and Engineering at the University of California, San Diego, where he is Co-Director of the Institute for Neural Computation.

Sejnowski coinvented the Boltzmann machine with Geoffrey Hinton and pioneered the application of learning algorithms to difficult problems in speech (NETtalk) and vision. His infomax algorithm for Independent Component Analysis (ICA) with Tony Bell has been widely adopted in machine learning, signal processing, and data mining. In 1989, he founded *Neural Computation*, which is the leading journal in neural networks and computational neuroscience and is published by the MIT Press. He is also the President of the Neural Information Processing Systems Foundation, a nonprofit organization that oversees the annual NIPS Conference. Terry is in a group of only twelve living scientists to have been elected to all three of the US national academies: sciences, medicine, and engineering.

Alistair McConville is the Director of Learning and Innovation at Bedales School in Hampshire, England. He studied Theology at Cambridge University before teaching Philosophy, Religious Studies, and Classics in several British independent schools. He has had an interest in neuroscience and education since getting involved with the Mind, Brain, and Education movement at Harvard in 2012. He has been published in their *Mind, Brain, and Education* journal and writes about educational matters more broadly for the *Times Educational Supplement.* He has spoken at a range of education conferences in the UK.

McConville is an independent schools inspector and school governor, and sits on the steering committee for Eton College's Innovation and Research Centre. He is an active participant in the Research Schools International movement, which works to link educational research with classroom practice. At Bedales School, he oversees a unique, progressive curriculum. He also raises pigs, bees, chickens, and three children. He now has a Chemistry General Certificate of Secondary Education (GCSE).

Oliver Young is a teacher of Design and Technology in English secondary schools, working with teenagers in a range of independent and state-funded institutions. After studying at St. Martin's School of Art in London, England, he worked in technical illustration before becoming an educator. He has had success in the F1 in Schools competition and has received the City and Guilds of London Institute's Computer Aided Design Parametric Modelling award. Young has appeared on TV's *Robot Wars* with a robot called Shellshock, and he has written articles about computer-aided design and manufacture for the Design and Technology Association's magazine *Designing.* He is an active member of the Association of Pole Lathe Turners and Green Woodworkers and author of the graphic novel *An Amoeba Called Joe.* He is also the coauthor of three children, supports Arsenal football club, and plays guitar in a rock band. Learn more about Oliver's work at oliveryoung.com.

Also by

Barbara Oakley, PhD

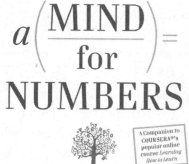

"A good teacher will leave you educated. But a great teacher will leave you curious. Well, Barbara Oakley is a great teacher. Not only does she have a mind for numbers, she has a way with words, and she makes every one of them count."
—Mike Rowe, creator and host of Discovery Channel's *Dirty Jobs* and CEO of mikeroweWORKS

a (MIND/for) = NUMBERS

A Companion to COURSERA®'s popular online course *Learning How to Learn*

HOW TO EXCEL AT MATH AND SCIENCE
(Even If You Flunked Algebra)

BARBARA OAKLEY, Ph.D.

Mindshift

Break Through Obstacles to Learning and Discover Your Hidden Potential

Barbara Oakley, PhD

Bestselling Author of A Mind for Numbers

And Creator of the Popular Massive Open Online Course "Learning How to Learn"

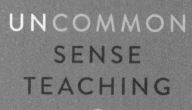

UNCOMMON
SENSE
TEACHING

Practical Insights in
Brain Science to
Help Students Learn

From the creators of the popular online course *Learning How to Learn*

Barbara Oakley, PhD; Beth Rogowsky, EdD;
Terrence J. Sejnowski, PhD

tarcherperigee